Create Demand and Stop Chasing Business: Secrets of a Top Real Estate Producer

By Ron Howard

Early Praise for *Create Demand and Stop Chasing Business*

"If I could recommend one Realtor to work with in Baltimore, it has to be Ron. If you want to represent any of the qualities that have made him successful over the years, you'll not only read this book but incorporate as many of his lessons as possible into your own life."
Joe Mechlinski, New York Times Bestselling Author of *Grow Regardless*

"This is less of a blueprint of what to do and more of a guide of how to shift into the Top Producer mindset. There is no Holy Grail of real estate; there is no secret system or plug-and-play for massive profit but follow the tenets in Ron's no-nonsense book, and success is assured. In my sixth month of real estate, I have eight active listings and seven settlements in May alone—thanks to his principles."
John Stockton, Realtor, RE/MAX Preferred

"Ron simply gets it. Branding creates a perception...a trust without a product, service, or person. Trust can't be built without the solid foundation created by great relationships. Ron's authenticity, his systems, and his ferocious drive to succeed are why he is one of the top real estate teams in the RE/MAX Network. For those looking for the roadmap, here it is. All you have to do is take action!"

Josh Bolgren, Region Executive Vice President, RE/MAX, LLC

"Ron is a real estate professional that sees communities to grow instead of buildings to sell. His passion for his local community and commitment of time and resources sets him apart from his competitors. Leaders in many fields will find great advice to recharge their own professional passion and commitment to excellence."

Jennifer Robinson, Executive Director of Friends of Patterson Park

"*Create Demand and Stop Chasing Business* is a phenomenal read and I could not put it down. Ron's "friends not funnels" and "think like a pilot" mentalities are brilliant. He reminds you that despite your intent the perception people have of you is what really matters. Ron is genuine. The relationships he creates are authentic, and he truly cares about what's best for his clients and friends. Reading this book is a MUST if you want to step up your game and build your own empire. Thank you for sharing your wisdom, Ron, you are truly the best of the best."

Emma Young, Sales & Marketing Manager New Home Construction

"If your goal is to "work smarter and not harder" all while loving what you do, then *Create Demand and Stop Chasing Business* is the perfect book for you. I have worked alongside Ron Howard and his team for over four years, and I have worked within the mortgage originating business for 15 years. It is without hesitation, I can say that Ron surpasses any other real estate professional. It's pure unselfishness that he has allowed us a snapshot into his thinking and an insight into his success. If you're looking for a guide to take your profession, regardless of what you do, to the next level, then this book is for you."

Amy L. Fichter, PRMI Branch Manager/Loan Originator

"WOW! If you are holding this book and thinking of starting a business...ANY business, I have one question for you. Do you want your business to "DIE OR NOT DIE?" If it is the latter, start reading immediately!"

Lawrence Gilliard Jr. *The Walking Dead,* HBO's *Deuce, Gangs of New York, The Wire*

"Not only did Ron create a great manual for success for real estate agents, but also for anyone who is interested in becoming the best in their craft. Ron is truly one of the hardest-working, laser focused, and community conscious real estate leaders I've worked with in my career. The ideas shared in this book are fresh and relevant to today's market, but also timeless in their underlying principles. Hard work, credibility, humility, and an authentic desire to give back are all essential keys to Creating Demand and standing out in the crowd. Thank you, Ron!"

Stuart Epstein, VP, George Mason Mortgage
Top Producing Lender

"Ron's impact on Baltimore has been immeasurable. His commitment to making Baltimore City a unique market for city dwellers is admirable. He has consistently worked to make downtown Baltimore a place that showcases and supports the arts. Due to his philanthropic work and by being the one of presenting sponsors over the years, WTMD's First Thursday music festival has enjoyed exponential growth and reached more people than ever before. For that we are grateful."

Andy Grimshaw, Sales Director WTMD 89.7

Create Demand and Stop Chasing Business:

Secrets of a Top Real Estate Producer

ISBN-13: 978-1717136237

ISBN-10: 1717136230

Cover design by Sooraj Mathew

Table of Contents

Dedication

Dedicated to my new wife, Jeni. Your patience throughout this process and constant support of my goals in life make it all worth celebrating.

Foreword

Ron Howard can not only hand you the keys to your dream home, but the answers to your pressing business goals. I assure you, *Create Demand and Stop Chasing Business* is not a boring business read. Ron delivers shock, humor, and head-nodding wisdom on every page.

The self-help genre is a crowded space filled with authors shouting advice from bookshelves. As a *New York Times* bestselling author, I know that the only books with a chance at survival are written with the reader at the forefront. *Create Demand and Stop Chasing Business* masters this.

Ron brings lessons and strategies that are relatable, implementable, and relevant regardless of your industry or niche. In a world where we are constantly being bombarded with enticements for the latest and greatest ways to generate business, it's refreshing to see Ron focus on simple yet powerful ideas that work.

With more than 15 years of experience in real estate—perhaps one of the most volatile markets in existence—Ron presents dynamic theories on relationship-building science, a no-funnels sales approach, and smart social media that will transform your brand and business.

As a business leader, it's your responsibility to create and foster meaningful connections that contribute to higher levels of engagement. After reading *Create Demand and Stop Chasing Business,* Ron's new mindset and perspective on business will make you stand out in the marketplace and empower you to achieve greater success through deeper connections with people that matter to you, your business, and your community.

-Joe Mechlinksi

New York Times bestselling author of *Grow Regardless,* CEO of SHIFT, speaker, and entrepreneur

Introduction

I was only 20 hours into flight school training when I took my first long-distance solo flight. Initially, I was excited and felt confident, but that had been 15 minutes ago when I'd still been on the ground. Now, I was up 4,000 feet, and couldn't see a thing. The surrounding fog suddenly and completely engulfed me, leaving the horizon a wishful dream. All my visual cues were gone, and I was dependent on instruments in the cockpit. At that moment, I felt lost, terrified, and on the verge of losing my mind. *How the hell was I ever going to get this plane, and myself, on the ground again*?

This experience up in the clouds—or should I say fog—was eerily reminiscent of how my life had been playing out just a few short months earlier. Then, too, I'd felt not only lost, but stressed, worried, and unsure about my future.

I had always been reasonably successful in life, generating just enough income each year to cover my ever-growing expenses. As a young man, I'd had a lot of fun, and a decent income certainly made it easier. I didn't think too much about savings. I was still in my early 30s and had a good track record of success. To me, retirement was a long way off.

Then it happened. I had my first game-changing setback. I miscalculated the funds I needed as I was closing a business. I'd never had a significant financial crisis until then, and it caught me off-guard. For the first time in my life, I'd put myself in a situation where I wasn't exactly sure what I was going to do next. But, as I reflect on this experience, it was a bit like losing myself up in the fog. All I knew was that I had to do something—and quick.

I remember sitting on my sofa wondering how it had all gone so terribly wrong.

I'm not one to flounder in self-pity, but it was pretty hard to avoid when I realized that one of the things that I had to do was sell my car to pay off some bills. At 34, I was flat broke. Fortunately, my girlfriend had a spare car, but lending it to me only reinforced her feeling that I was a loser. Before long she was gone, too.

As I sat alone thinking about my future, memories filled my head, but one stood out.

I was 14 and had just moved to Maryland from Hawaii. I was unfocused and didn't know anyone. On the first day at my new school, the wrestling coach approached me. Mike Hampe was a well-known and respected coach who had received many accolades. He was slim in build, wore glasses, and had a thick head of hair.

"Son," he said to me with a friendly smile, "have you ever thought about wrestling?"

I hadn't, but he didn't give me time to reply.

"I think it would be good for you," he said. "What do you think?"

"What does it involve?" I asked.

"Getting in the best physical and mental shape of your life."

"Sounds like a lot of hard work."

"No, it isn't hard work," the coach replied.

I looked at him with suspicion.

"It's beyond hard work. It's going to take a massive effort," he said emphasizing “massive” and “effort.”

"Hard work can only get you so far. Massive effort will get you to the top," he finished convincingly.

That encounter with Coach Hampe transformed my life. With his help, I learned about the level above hard work and the massive effort that propelled my wrestling, life, and self-esteem.

As I sat alone on that couch, I knew that nothing less than a massive effort was going to work to get me out of my situation, and I was ready to embrace it.

That crisis was the kind of stumble in life we all might go through at some point or another. Instead of feeling sorry for myself, the pressure of going broke and getting dumped created one of those pivotal moments in my life where I changed *everything*. I had few outside distractions and the chance to genuinely take stock of myself. With Coach's advice ringing in my ears, I achieved fantastic clarity around my next moves, a deep honesty with myself, and I knew I had the grit required to give a genuine 110% effort. Going broke forced me to *go* for broke. I dedicated myself to not just getting out of the hole I was in but starting a successful real estate business.

I became the change that my life needed.

I understood sales and had a history of being a hard worker, so I usually had 20 tasks going on at once. But going broke made the music, noise, and everything else stop, so I could focus intently on what I needed to do to launch my business as a real estate agent. During that time on the sofa, I came up with simple, yet powerful ideas that eventually catapulted me into real estate and back into the big blue skies.

I had business-to-business sales experience, but I knew selling and connecting with consumers was going to be a whole different ballgame that required a different approach. To me it seemed simple: Learn how to position myself as a go-to Realtor without chasing people, make as many connections as possible, and figure out ways to make people want to hire me when they were ready to buy or sell.

Fast forward 13 years to 2017: My sales team is continually one of the top RE/MAX teams nationwide. Last year, we completed 533 transactions, topped $155 million in sales and generated nearly $4 million in commissions. We're beginning to move into new metro markets. Our 650+ Zillow reviews tell us we're doing service the right way.

This book started out as the answer to a question one of my agents asked me: *What are the top things you do better than most?* To answer that question, I had to go back in time to when I was broke. To recover, I had no choice but to give my business and my life 110 percent. That is when I made a lot of my discoveries that I share with you today. As you progress through this book, you will learn to stop wasting money on training you will never use. I'll teach you a few strategies that will help build your business, elevate yourself and the industry in your community, and make people want to work with you one after another.

If a regular guy like me, who started out broke, dumped and carless sitting on a couch with barely two nickels to rub together can get off the ground and pull this off, so can you.

After endless hours articulating into actionable takeaways, I'm proud to share *Create Demand and Stop Chasing Business* with you.

Thank you for reading.

Ron Howard
Spring 2017
Baltimore, Md.

Keep learning at: createdemandandstopchasing.com

Chapter 1

Lost in the Crowd

"We cannot solve our problems with the same thinking we used when we created them."
-Albert Einstein

For many Realtors, it takes some time to shift from an employee mindset to a *holy-shit-I'm-a-small-business-owner-who-needs-to-make-some-sales-quickly-or-I'll-be-back-at-my-dead-end-job-in-no-time* survivor mindset. I've seen similar confusion when a new homeowner calls to tell me their AC just went out as if I was their landlord. After renting over the years, they're programmed to call someone for their problems. I've had the *hey-you're-a-homeowner-now-you-need-to-call-the-repair-man,* conversation more times than I can count. As a Realtor, you've got to know how to call the shots for your small business, just as a new homeowner has to learn how to fix their leaky pipes...or know who to call. And for any new or rebranded agents, remember, the massive effort you must put into your first three months will help define your next six months.

Being a small business owner means juggling as you learn the Realtor craft, spreading the word about your business, finding clients, and applying a laundry list of other tactics that go into generating transactions. However, stress-inducing this growing list becomes, the good news is that there's no shortage of companies that want to sell you something to help you succeed in any of these areas. The bad news? You'll be bombarded with endless offers for training, coaching, websites, leads, and all sorts of stuff that is often dated, doesn't work anymore, or never really worked that well in the first place. We've all attended courses or seminars run by supposed "realty business gurus" only to find ourselves at the end of an expensive and time-consuming event left with the same *go-chase-some-business* ideas. Recently, I sat through a mind-numbing day of training. Twenty minutes into it, after hearing the one original idea he had, the trainer went into the same ol' regurgitated door-knocking, cold-calling ideas I've heard hundreds of times before. We received a survey at the end of the day, and one of the questions read: "What are your thoughts on the execution of the trainer?" I thought *I'd be okay with that.*

In this book, I'll share with you dozens of ideas that grew my business without having to chase business. But, there are countless other things you will need to do to succeed as a real estate agent. Other lead-generating activities include pay-per-click advertising, Facebook promotions, and the development of strong referral partners, each just as helpful as the next when it comes to generating sales. Since launching my business, it has grown by *not doing* what a lot of seminars and courses teach you is a great way to gain success as a Realtor: chase business.

Even though a lot of the industry stars pushed training that focused on chase-type activities like cold-calling, door-knocking or going after expired listings, I didn't know many agents who were actually successful at chasing business. The few who were seemed to have model good looks and a super smooth game. It was like the business chased *them*. This type of training never resonated with me, and as an average guy who stuttered from time to time, I felt I lacked the natural skills that chasing business required. I also wanted to have a great quality of life as I grew my business. That's important to me, and most would feel the same way. Pursuing people all over town didn't appear to be the best way to do that.

I knew I had to figure out a different and better way to generate clients.

Between lead gen and website companies, brokerages, training gurus, and tech solution companies pitching us the next best thing, we need to weed through that crowded space to find ideas to make our business grow. The marketers in our industry are pros at exciting us and making us temporarily lose our minds and so we buy training we end up never using. We've all fallen victim to these flashy gimmicks where we end up with an entire graveyard of barely used or ineffective training material on our shelves. Companies keep selling outdated training because we keep buying it. Later in this book, I'll let you in on the same tactics that marketers use to get you to pull the trigger to buy stuff you probably don't need and most likely will never use.

Consumers have grown savvier with the help of online reviews and are funnel weary from being constantly sold to. Everyone, (save for a few seniors who were raised to be politer), hate getting cold-called, door-knocked, or prospected. Most of us have no problem ignoring numbers we don't recognize and don't hesitate to hang up. The fact is, unsolicited approaches to the public are likely to alienate many more people than they will add to your transaction count. In a recent study, for example, almost half the people surveyed said that a company's intrusive social media ads frustrate them to the point that they vow never to buy from them and publicly badmouth them. Old-school habits die hard in today's world.

Not only is the hard-closing, overly-scripted, and pushy salesperson a thing of the past, it's something most of us Realtors wouldn't be good at even if we wanted to be. Since the start of my real estate career, I've stayed away from the chase and pressure tactics, the overly-scripted conversations, and outdated closing techniques. I've found more authentic ways to connect with people, develop real relationships, and create demand for my services.

Getting to the Front of the Pack

As a new Realtor, it's tough to position yourself immediately to get hired. The hardest and most critical time to get your first real estate gig is within the first few months. To rank against the big leagues, the veterans in the industry who have honed their craft for decades, and me...you've got to hit the ground running. (No pressure.)

I've found being thought of as a go-to agent and getting hired was the biggest challenge I faced right out of the gate. Every agent professes they are the best, but I didn't see much effort from agents in creating a brand that stood for loftier ideals. I knew if I crafted a brand that genuinely represented noble concepts and could somehow inject that into the minds of the people around me, I would have a greater chance of quickly getting hired.

I asked myself this question:

"If you were in the market for a Realtor, would you hire yourself or one of the other top five agents you already know?"

I was disappointed with my honest answer of *Hell no.* There wasn't anything unique about me that would make me competitive with top Realtors. I had to make immediate changes. I knew it would be difficult for people to hire me if I wouldn't even hire myself.

The fact is, whether you accept the notion of branding or not, you project an image that significantly influences people's perceptions of you. Putting in zero effort still gives you a brand, just not a very good one. So, don't allow yourself to be like the thousands of other Realtors who don't understand branding, perception, and the impact it has on their businesses. You'll get lost in the endless sea of agents with a nice logo, but not much else.

For one thing, you could be misperceiving your brand. Self-image is often misleading. You might see yourself as a compassionate, hard-working guy or gal with a lot of interests, but others might see you as half-assed and spread too thin. You might think of yourself as frank and honest, but others might see you as hard-nosed and a poor listener. The differences you present to the world can be subtle, yet they may make a critical impact on other people.

Our biggest problem starting out is how do we get people to hire us, and quickly? To do so requires taking a long look at yourself and using honest reflection. It takes a massive effort to discover new and potentially transformative aspects of yourself that attract people and make them want to work with you. This challenge led me to some unique ideas that made instant and huge impressions on my business.

The image you present has to be memorable and desirable. Your brand will not be effective if nobody remembers it and it won't work if nobody wants what you're offering. Your brand, or lack thereof, can either put you at the front or the back of the pack.

A New Way of Thinking

To give this real estate game 110% effort, we need new and better strategies to make it work.

Most of us decide to give our business everything we've got and do whatever is necessary. But doing this requires new skills: focus, attention, better decision-making, stress management, prioritization, ignoring distractions, and mental toughness to name a few. Several other factors influence your ability to maintain the focus, energy, and everything else needed to develop your best self.

First, if you're going to develop the *right* mindset, some old habits have to go. They slow down your progress and have a negative impact on the quality of work you need to produce to grow a successful business. Carving out a new routine requires action, so you can't quietly tell yourself you're going to change and expect it just to happen. Understand what you're trying to do, have a realistic plan to achieve it, and keep up the motivation to implement new behaviors long enough so that they become a part of you.

In addition to the fact that most people aren't prepared for or don't know how to make critical changes, life conspires to distract us, stress us out, and generally keep us off balance.

While putting massive effort into my branding, I stumbled upon a new type of mindset and way of thinking applicable to about every real estate situation I've experienced. The results were immediate and changed my life in so many ways. I'll tell you all about it in Chapter 4.

If I'm Not Chasing Leads; What am I Doing?

In striving to make real connections, I had to shift the focus from a sales funnel mindset to building genuine relationships with no expectation of a sale. *Without the selling and closing mentality, how can you influence people to hire you?*

I hate to admit that a notable trait in our industry is an agent's ability to recite scripts that result in disingenuous communication and superficial relationships with clients. To many, scripts are the Holy Grail, designed to make you think their magic words will instantly convert your prospect into a client. Reciting lines, closing routines, and adding people to pipelines and sales funnels seems to be more important than having a sincere interest in building real relationships. I know some people are great at selling in this manner, and that's awesome, but I believed there was a better way.
We get so caught up in the selling mindset that we forget about the relationship mindset. We monitor our words,

using specific phrases we have been taught that will have our prospects instantly in the palm of our hands. But in truth, bringing in clients with those tactics hardly ever works like that. I'll let you in on some better practices that can influence a person's decision-making, without having to put them in an old-school closing routine.

I went on a vision quest to get better at connecting, persuading, triggering and influencing people to want to use my services. No chase, no sell, just better connection. What I found was transformative.

Making More Friends

I knew that I needed to authentically develop a larger sphere of influence and find ways to relate to those folks, so they would naturally see me as the go-to Realtor when they were ready. I needed to figure out a way to get more people to hire me without chasing after them!

Because the pursuit of relationships can be misguided and ill-informed, you might end up being perceived as an overly-ambitious social climber, or an irritating bother forcing your way into new social circles. Or, if you're mostly focused on buying leads, you may be seen as someone who has a lot of e-mail addresses, but not a large database of people willing to hire you.

It's not the size of the database, but the quality that counts. Look, anyone can capture e-mails and phone numbers. Right out of the gate, I thought that the key to growth was developing a personal relationship with as many people as I could. However, most of the training and focus in our industry nowadays is on generating and converting leads. Lead generation and conversion are super important, but if you don't want to chase business, you'll have to grow your sphere of influence in a smart, healthy, and authentic way.

Developing a great personal network, as opposed to chasing business, takes a unique strategy, commitment and time. As a result, many Realtors ignore this essential aspect of their business and end up wondering why they only made $42,000 last year.

I developed a simple system that will add hundreds of people a year to your sphere, elevate you in your community, and launch the sustained growth of your business without chasing it. Stay tuned.

Doing Social Media Right

The advent of social media has made it seem that building a sphere of influence has never been easier, but that's a misconception. Social media can present more problems than it can provide solutions. For one thing, social media can amplify your brand, and if that's not as strong as it should be, you will have problems. Social media should also be used in the right way. You can ruin your reputation with one click. In fact, although this seems obvious, I have seen way too many Realtors and other professionals significantly dent, if not ruin, their standing in the community with undisciplined social media posts.

Again, this doesn't mean you should steer clear of Twitter, Facebook, or LinkedIn, but you need to understand how to use these tools to help you, not hurt you.

Getting Ready for Flight

Most of us get overwhelmed with how to get more transactions faster, and how to prioritize tasks associated with setting up business and finding technology that works.

Picking the wrong route or the wrong technology to invest in can stall you before you ever get off the ground.

The few agents that break out into success get so busy it becomes difficult to go back and set up their business the way it should have been from the get-go.

I'll share with you a simple idea to get off the ground fast, set your business up right, and pick the technology that works well.

In the following chapters, I will provide you with a few practical pointers that will help you: Develop a brand that stands out, learn a new mindset, understand relationship-building science, attract good people, implement concepts big marketers use through social media, and get your business off the ground fast. If you use only a few of the ideas, your business will be impacted greatly.

RULES FROM THE CROWD:

- You're a small business, act like one.
- If you're not going to chase business, stop buying programs that teach you to do that.
- You'll never become a "go-to" agent through causal efforts.
- To make 110% effort work, you'll need the right mindset.
- Most of us hate being sold to.
- If you're not chasing business, you're going to need an alternative route to success.
- Social media is probably hurting you more than it is helping.

Keep learning at: createdemandandstopchasing.com

Chapter 2

Base Training

"Problem-solving leaders have one thing in common: a faith that there's always a better way."
-Gerald M. Weinberg

In the last chapter, I told you the problems I saw in real estate when I was starting out. There may be that 1-in-20 Realtor who makes chasing business work, but the rest of us normal folk need other ways to hit big numbers. I put these ideas to work for me by exerting massive effort into certain areas of my life, which led to an entire range of great results. Some of these ideas can work for you!

Even though my sales team, Ron Howard & Associates, has more than a decade of strong business growth based on my unique approach, I've stayed out of the "tell-all" game of writing a book. Until now. Since I've surpassed 500+ annual transactions, I'm ready to share some ideas and beliefs that generate a lot of business without chasing it.

My ideas compare to what wins races for endurance athletes: good base training. When I used to mountain bike race, base training was one of the hardest concepts to grasp and implement. It seemed counterintuitive to train slowly to get faster later in our season, but the winners know it's the only way to end up at the top of the podium. A lot of athletes don't put in enough base training and go straight to high-intensity workouts. But this doesn't build the necessary aerobic endurance, so their stamina doesn't last. Similarly, many Realtors jump right into the business without developing a good base layer of concepts that work. They get spread too thin trying anything and everything under the sun to generate more business.

Branding: It Matters What People Think of You

Simply put, branding is the perception the general public, and your market, have of you. You and your business are a brand, whether you like it or not. Your goal should be to develop attributes that separate you from the pack and to build trust through your actions and behavior. It takes self-reflection and development of the ability to see the big picture (past, present, future) to change or improve your brand. There is a high cost of having a bad brand and a great reward for a good one. I'm going to show you how I put massive effort into four branding ideas that instantly elevated me to becoming a go-to Realtor in my market and that launched a few business discoveries that have led to positive growth over the years.

High-Performance Mindset

Giving a true 110% to a new job or business requires adopting a mindset that will make it work. I had lived my life by being ambitious enough to get by and have fun, but when you flip the *let's-make-shit-happen* switch, you'll need a new set of rules for how you think.

Esteemed Stanford University Psychologist, Carol Dweck, explains in *Mindset: The New Science of Success* how Michael Jordan became the successful athlete we all know. Instead of quitting after being cut from his high school basketball team, Jordan took his setback as an opportunity to work harder than anyone else in the world. After six years, his initiative earned him the cover shot of *Sports Illustrated* with the caption, "A Star is Born."

This wasn't a fluke. Michael Jordan implemented what Dweck calls, a "growth mindset," where he believed through hard work and dedication, he was going to improve enough to make it to the NBA. Simply put, you can either believe that you can continue to develop your skills, or you have a "fixed mindset." The key to incorporating a growth mindset into your life is recognizing that failure is a part of learning.

I wasn't able to find real estate training that taught how to achieve a performance or growth mindset, but Michael Jordan didn't exactly have a list of instructions either. Obviously, I'm no Michael Jordan, but we both saw problems and sought the solutions to figure them out. Initially, no one in my market seemed to be performance-oriented. The typical agent rolled in around 10 a.m., and it looked as though the top producers in my market had been in the right place at the right time to benefit from market upswings. To my eyes, it was a casual pursuit of business.

I had four branding ideas when I started, and one was to be seen as "sharp like a pilot." That branding idea led me to about a dozen new ways to mentally approach and complement my effort to give life and business 110% effort.

Influence and Connect Like a Jedi

I'll never forget a field trip I took to see *Star Wars* in the third grade when I attended Santa Barbara Catholic School in Guam. We weren't Catholic, but my parents thought the discipline would help keep me focused. As a nine-year-old, I was blown away, and from that moment on, imagined myself as a Jedi...who didn't? Any time situations worked out my way, and I was unclear exactly as to how I had pulled it off, I was certain my success had been due to my Jedi mind tricks.

At times, I'm sure we've all felt like a Jedi, especially when an appraiser comes in with the highest valuation in the neighborhood. You meet with the appraiser with the sole goal to make a connection, influence them to like you, and try to get the best value. So, it definitely feels like a favor from The Force when, against all odds, the value comes in.

I've met plenty of Realtors I would never hire, who didn't exactly put off the "I'm a financial professional" vibe. Whether they were overdramatic, sloppy, or unprofessional, they never had a chance to sell me on their capabilities. They presented and lost the sale, simply by being who they are.

I had to find a way to create the exact *opposite* effect with clients and find real-life techniques to connect better and more authentically with people to get them to want to hire me. These were real-life Jedi mind tricks. I will show you some cool stuff to consider when forming the best version of your business self, and the super powerful ways to connect with the subconscious...lightsabers optional.

Developing a Huge Network

Since I wasn't going to cold-call, door-knock, and prospect to find clients, my biggest challenge would be figuring out how to increase my sphere of influence that would hire or refer me. In this game, business is often gained not by *what* you know, but *who*. Your social network can become the key driver of your business. If you connect too infrequently, people will forget you. If you connect too often, you'll smother them. So, how do you build your sphere of influence without looking like an overly-anxious social climber trying to insert yourself into bigger and better circles? Pushing yourself into new crowds will work for a few, but the trick is to be invited. How do you get people to want to be around you? How do you get them to want to connect with you? That is the challenge.

Developing a huge sphere of influence the right way has been one of the keys to my team's success. I will show you a simple process to make people want to be in your social circle in Chapter 6.

A Social Media Strategy Guide

Social media offers plenty of opportunities to build your brand. You can create brand awareness with your target audience, stay in touch with current clients, capture leads, and so much more.

But then there's the flip side of the coin; the fact that these powerful tools are right at your fingertips, letting you easily damage, cripple, or even kill your brand and reputation. I regularly watch agents thin the "Realtor herd" and throw their chances of ever building a successful brand out the window after posting the most moronic updates on social media.

Your online reputation will help make or break your business. Stop being a social media drag aka stop posting constant self-promotion, never-ending complaints, and negativity. My simple strategies will enhance your social media presence and help you generate more business. Use my social media rules, and you'll create more lift for your business.

Getting off the Ground Fast

As a new agent, you're trying to learn a ton of info at a hyper-fast pace. It's incredibly tough to figure how to prioritize what you need to do next.

I generally see three types of entries in our business.

1) New agents get their license and business cards and slowly try and find their way. They reach out to friends, toy with buying leads and inevitably get lost in the crowd without ever cashing in huge commissions.

2) New agents crash and burn. They fly full throttle into the business, promoting themselves as a real estate expert even though they've never done one deal. This group quickly finds out how the business works. People who want to sell a house, call a friend who has been a Realtor for 10 years. They don't risk doing the deal with a brand-new agent. These types flash for a quick minute on social media, before realizing it's a lot of hard work to run their business. They fizzle out and disappear back to their old industries.

3) New agents that do the research, put the time in, read the books, take the training and run their business like a business. They get everything in order before going full throttle. This is the smallest group of the three.

I'll share with you a simple method I used to get to 10 transactions in my third month, give you some great tips on how to set up your business and share with you the technology that we use to run our business.

This book and its solutions are an alternate route to achieving high volume in sales without going door-to-door. I'll walk you through each of the core ideas I've developed in the following chapters. These include massive effort branding, adopting a performance mindset, science-based tactics to build relationships, growing your sphere with people that want to be in it, implementing an easy-to-understand social media formula and getting off the ground fast. For me, the core ideas had an immediate impact right out of the gate, and I know you'll find the same results.

RONS RULES FROM THE BASE:

- Focus on creating demand, and you can stop chasing business.
- Put massive effort into your branding, and it will make you stand out.
- Adopt a performance mindset and give 110% effort.

- Understand simple relationship-building science to help you connect better.
- Focus on friendships and not sales funnels to help you build your sphere.
- Use simple rules to make your social media help and not hurt you.
- Get off the ground fast with simple ideas and smart choices.

Keep learning at: createdemandandstopchasing.com

Chapter 3

Massive Effort Branding

"Your brand is what other people say about you when you're not in the room."

-Jeff Bezos

Mention the word "branding," and most people picture mega-million-dollar campaigns by Coke, Nike, or Apple. Their minds conjure up logos, social media campaigns, or some repetitive jingle from a commercial they can't get out of their heads.

But presenting a brand isn't just for the big boys. So why don't more Realtors realize what good branding can do?

Like I mentioned in Chapter 1, very few of us think of ourselves as small business owners who need to stand out in a crowded field. Instead, the first thing we're taught is to chase business right out of the gate, to run through scripts, to make as many touches as possible through our sphere of influence. As a result, too many people jump into real estate and slam down the gas pedal hard before they fully understand the product they're selling.

But before you hit the ground running, have you put any thought into who you *think* you are? More importantly, who you want to be? Are you seen as a star, a smart ass, a genius or an idiot? Are you, kind, empathetic, caring, or psychotic? What about trustworthy, honest, fair, or a cheat? The list goes on. But the point is that marketers have figured out that other people's perceptions of you affect their attitude and willingness to engage with you.

Perception is important, so you need to consider what impression you want to make on others and then find ways of conveying it. The fact that this appears to be a contrived and conscious effort turns people off from wanting to brand themselves. The truth is, the way you portray yourself is an important factor in all your relationships, especially your business ones.

As a Realtor or any professional, your product is you.

Creating or reinventing your brand should make hiring you a no-brainer when people in your network are ready to buy or sell. In my market, everyone knows at least five agents. The trick is to create a brand image that makes people pick me and not them.

People resist the notion of branding because they think it'll turn them into an unnatural version of themselves. Don't fake it.

Your goal is to create the **best version** of yourself, **not an unnatural version** of yourself.

People can generally spot fakers a long way off, and while they may ignore them in small matters, they are certainly not going to consider working with a fraud in their most important financial and personal transactions. The worst thing is to be inauthentic. It reeks of lying, cheating, and posing. I learned this lesson as a young boy.

I shared with you that I was a party-goer, and how it hurt my brand. Maybe you have different behaviors to address? Stay away from making impressions that hurt your chances of working with new people. Avoid: being a cheater, liar, bad friend, self-centered, obnoxious, loud, rude, pain in the ass, troublemaker or drama king/queen.

Even the appearance of being a soccer mom/dad versus a full-time agent can prevent people from interacting with you. A lot of Realtors engage in rehabbing. If you are one of them, ask yourself if a potential client might see you as distracted. How do people perceive you?

When I was a kid in Hawaii, surfing was a big deal, obviously.

I'll admit, I was never a great surfer. I was okay, nothing great, but I could ride waves. Growing up in that surf culture made it pretty easy to pick out the posers before they even touched the water. They had all the expensive gear their parents had bought them and spent a ton of time on the beach posturing and waxing their boards. They dawdled getting into the water, then stayed there for the rest of the day, flopping around and not catching any waves. But hey, at least they looked good on the beach, right? These guys spent so much effort on their *surf guy* image before they could even ride a wave; thus, earning their poser label. The image they promoted wasn't authentic, and they were the laughingstock of the local surf tribe.

Authenticity will raise your stock, faking it will make you a laughing stock.

You earn your brand. Each facet is built, brick by brick, over a long period of time or with an extensive amount of effort. So even if you find a part of yourself that's flawed, this book will help you with the steps needed to rebrand.

If you're not prepared to create that best version of yourself, or your best version of yourself is not an image consistent with attracting customers, you might want to consider a different career path. Even if you decide to seek employment elsewhere, know that your image always goes with you. Wherever you go, there you are.

Fixing Your Brand

Traits to Drop	Traits to Adopt
Abrasive	Accessible
Abrupt	Adaptable
A crook	Admirable
Angry	Adventurous
Annoying	Agreeable

Traits to Drop	**Traits to Adopt**
Argumentative	Amiable
Arrogant	Appreciative
Careless	Articulate
Childish	Balanced
Cold	Brilliant
Complacent	Calm
Conceited	Capable
Crass	Captivating
Criminal	Caring
Crude	Charismatic
Cruel	Charming
Cynical	Cheerful
Deceitful	Compassionate
Demanding	Confident
Desperate	Considerate
Destructive	Cooperative
Devious	Courageous
Difficult	Courteous
Dirty	Creative
Discouraging	Cultured
Discourteous	Curious

Traits to Drop	Traits to Adopt
Dishonest	Decent
Disloyal	Decisive
Disobedient	Dedicated
Disorganized	Dignified
Disrespectful	Disciplined
Disruptive	Dynamic
Disturbing	Educated
Domineering	Efficient
Drama King/Queen	Elegant
Dull	Energetic
Erratic	Enthusiastic
Flamboyant	Exciting
Foolish	Extraordinary
Forgetful	Fair
Fraudulent	Farsighted
Frightening	Flexible
Frivolous	Focused
Greedy	Forceful
Hateful	Friendly
Haughty	Fun-Loving
Hostile	Generous
Ignorant	Gentle

Traits to Drop	Traits to Adopt
Impatient	Genuine
Impractical	Giving
Inconsiderate	Good-Natured
Insecure	Gracious
Insensitive	Hardworking
Insincere	Healthy
Insulting	Helpful
Lazy	Honest
Malicious	Honorable
Messy	Humble
Miserable	Humorous
Moody	Idealistic
Narcissistic	Imaginative
Narrow-Minded	Incorruptible
Obnoxious	Innovative
Opinionated	Insightful
Opportunistic	Intelligent
Paranoid	Intuitive
Pain in the Ass	Kind
Petty	Logical
Pompous	Lovable
Pretentious	Loyal

Traits to Drop	Traits to Adopt
Resentful	Mature
Ridiculous	Meaningful
Sadistic	Modest
Selfish	Objective
Shallow	Observant
Shortsighted	Open
Sloppy	Optimistic
Slow	Organized
Small-Thinking	Original
Stiff	Passionate
Superficial	Patient
Suspicious	Peaceful
Tactless	Perceptive
Tasteless	Perfectionist
Thoughtless	Personable
Unappreciative	Persuasive
Uncaring	Polished
Uncharitable	Practical
Uncooperative	Precise
Undisciplined	Principled
Unfriendly	Profound
Ungrateful	Protective

Traits to Drop

Unpolished

Unprincipled

Unrealistic

Unreliable

Unrestrained

Unstable

Vague

Venomous

Vindictive

You're an Asshole

Traits to Adopt

Punctual

Purposeful

Rational

Realistic

Reflective

Relaxed

Reliable

Resourceful

Respectful

Responsible

Responsive

Selfless

Self-Critical

Self-Defacing

Self-Sufficient

Serious

Sharing

Sharp

Simple

Skillful

Sociable

Solid

<u>Traits to Adopt</u>

Stable

Steadfast

Steady

Strong

Sympathetic

Systematic

Tasteful

Thorough

Tolerant

Trusting

Understanding

Warm

Well-Read

Well-Rounded

Witty

Youthful

*Thanks to Ideonomy for their help with this list.

Mirror, Mirror...

Figuring out your brand is really figuring out who you *want to be*. You'll need to take a hard look at your life and be honest about what you see, which isn't easy. Not only do we have bullshit beliefs about ourselves, but we are also invested in certain behaviors and views because they are comfortable for us. For example, I used to have a very active social life. I assumed that if I worked hard, I deserved to enjoy myself to the highest degree. But sitting on the couch that tough day, I realized people aren't likely to entrust one of their biggest financial transactions to a guy they had seen out partying at 2 am. I knew that part of my behavior had to change.

Think about this: The perception you want to create is the one that is consistent with what people want, i.e., getting the best deal they can on their house. Understandably, they want the best deal, and they don't want to worry about getting ripped off. So, they need to perceive you as honest, fair, hardworking, knowledgeable, smart, and diligent. One mistake we can make is to assume that general qualities of popularity, such as likable, fun, easy-going, are enough. While being likable *is* important, you wouldn't choose a surgeon who is cool, funny, and handsome, over the one who is smart and experienced. Don't get me wrong, the cool and handsome surgeon could also be smart and experienced, but if he doesn't project those qualities, no one will know. Which brings us to a second key point about branding.

It's one thing to develop a set of defining attributes, but it's another actually to demonstrate them. People don't know what they can't see.

As you think about your brand, you'll need to examine your preconceptions about who you are and what you're doing under the clear light of day. What version of yourself do you present?

Looking back, being flat broke was a great stroke of luck. That hard stare into the mirror made me realize I *wasn't* the best version of myself. I knew I could overcome my status with a massive effort to recreate myself, or to put it another way, if I branded *who I was.*

I came to understand that the life I had led to that point couldn't continue. My branding was kind of a self-transformation as well as the first layer of the foundation I laid out for my new business.

I knew being social could benefit my new business, but realized I had to stop doing the hard partying if I was ever going to be taken seriously and trusted. I wasn't presenting the version of myself consistent with attracting business. I couldn't be that carefree guy anymore; I had to change. It had to be so obvious, and dramatic that my old friends and acquaintances would have noticed the difference.

At that time, "brand" translated into, "getting your shit together." I had to understand what image needed to be presented, adopt the behaviors to reinforce the image, and act in accordance with it. Then, I had to get in front of as many people as possible, so they could see who I really was. That was a huge part—who I *really* was. This wasn't about role-playing the right behaviors, every action I took supported the goal of becoming *that* go-to Realtor.

When I started to turn my life around on that couch, I decided my brand was going to publicize me as the hardest working agent, who was heavily community-oriented, a great friend, and who was not thought of as a salesperson but was instead, sharp like a pilot. I'll explain that last idea in a bit.

Four Ideas with Huge Impact

Flying Toward Success

A few months before starting in real estate, a highly respected friend of mine had become a pilot. I was so impressed; I immediately decided a part of my new brand would be geared toward influencing people to think of me as *sharp like a pilot*. If I gave off that impression, then it would exceed any other mental barriers they might have in hiring me. When you think of the perception of a pilot, various qualities come to mind: smart, courageous, solid, dependable, reliable, willing to take on responsibility, and cool under fire. Those were definitely consistent with the qualities I wanted to convey and own. It was over the top, but I knew it would instantly position me as a sharp guy and the type of agent I would hire.

Soon enough, I signed up for flight school and earned my pilot's license six months later. I initially thought I was going to kill myself trying, but I didn't care, I still had that massive effort mindset kicking in and, thankfully, after the eighth lesson, I settled into the notion that I probably wasn't going to die.

I'll discuss in the next chapter how flight school inadvertently led me to develop a new mindset, put forth powerful ideas on how to look at everything differently, and handle my day-to-day performance and decision-making.

I want to impart that you don't have to go to flight school to find fresh inspiration for the new you. Flight school is an extreme example. There are all sorts of interesting hobbies that can shine a better light on your life. Learn a musical instrument or language, paint, become a yoga instructor, write a book, take cooking lessons, learn how to make furniture. Whatever you decide to do, when you find what works for you, you can base the foundation of the new you on a talent that most will find interesting and impressive.

Hardest Working Guy in Show Business

I thought people would consider hiring me if I became known as the hardest working agent in my market. I immediately stopped hitting the bars. Stopped dating. Stopped drinking. Stopped making quips and telling dry jokes, which confused people as often as it amused them. I completely disappeared for a while, so that I could push the reset button.

With my new free time, I started my day at the office at 5 a.m., worked until 7 a.m., then I would knock out two hours of flight school, and come back to the office around 9:30 a.m. Even doing this, I still beat most of the other agents. To project the image of the hardest working guy in the business, I *became* the hardest working guy in the business.

Getting Involved in the Community

As I scoped out the competition, I didn't see much community involvement from other agents. But I hadn't spent much time volunteering for anything, either. One successful agent stood out with a laundry list of his involvement in the community, his church, and all sorts of other types of volunteer work. So, I instantly wanted to be like that guy. I was already putting out the hardest-working, and sharp-like-a-pilot vibes, but felt that if someone were making a hiring decision based on community involvement, that other guy would be hired every single time. I put in a massive effort to get involved with as many nonprofits as possible.

A Better Friend

A lot of Realtors tend to get hired based on their personal relationships, regardless of how sharp, hardworking, or giving they are. I had a small circle of friends that were close and a much larger group of cordial acquaintances. If I wanted to make better connections, I'd have to figure out what made someone likable enough to get hired.

My desire to become a better friend led to a variety of meaningful lessons on connecting, persuading, triggering, and influencing people. I was fascinated with the underlying principles and theories that influenced people's subconscious to like or dislike, hire or not hire. To some of you who just jumped right into this business, that all might sound crazy. But putting in that massive effort to create a unique brand made me stand out clearly.

You don't need to become a pilot to give off a sharp impression. When you develop a strong brand, you will go an incredibly long way in attracting people to *want to work* with you.

By the time I launched my real estate career, I had become a completely different person because of my quest to compete and stand out from the pack. I became the best version of myself. In the short run, my first few weeks were an amazing time of reconnecting with everyone I knew as *The New Ron*. Everyone was interested in what I had been doing. It's hard to point to one idea that worked better than the others, but by giving massive effort at every opportunity, I had 10 deals under contract in my third month, and never looked back.

Drop 5/Add 5

Here's an exercise I've developed that might help you scare up some branding ideas. It's based on something I do each year. I call it the Drop 5/Add 5.

List five negative traits about yourself that might lead a prospect to hire someone else. Before I started, my five were:

1. I partied too much
2. I drank too much
3. I was too self-centered
4. I hung with the party crowd
5. I didn't project myself to be a financial professional

Then, dedicate to dropping those five traits—and stick to it. It might be hard at first, but it will turn you into a better and more successful person.

After making your Drop 5 list, do the opposite. List five traits you can adapt to enhance your brand. My five were:

1. Become the hardest working agent
2. Be sharp like a pilot
3. Give back to the community
4. Be a better friend
5. Connect with people who give back

If you don't trust yourself to be critical enough, send a Drop 5/Add 5 survey to five friends. Ask them to tell you the five traits they think you need to overcome to get more real estate business and another five that you could add to help you become a go-to.

You'll be amazed by what you learn from this exercise. Your big picture will help you discover what kind of person you think you are, how others see you, what they want from you, and how you want to be seen. Expect quite a few surprises. Embrace them. Negative feedback is a gift. It can expose blind spots and lead to necessary improvement. That's how you'll shape a brand that truly represents your best self.

5 Secrets to "Big Brand" Branding

1. Put massive effort into defining and becoming your brand. My descriptive definitions are "I'm sharp like a pilot;" "I'm the hardest working Realtor;" "I'm a caring friend," and "I give back to the community."
2. Make a good brand promise that evokes feelings. Rolex offers feelings of prestige. Corvette offers feelings of excitement. What feeling(s) do you evoke?
3. Make your brand (aka you) unique, and own it.
4. Your brand is not something you make up on a lunch break. It will require massive effort and a deep understanding of your competitors and marketplace.
5. Constantly manage your brand (who you are) and stay true to who you have become.

RON'S RULES FOR YOUR BRAND:

- Recreating yourself takes massive effort. Put in the time and energy.
- Convert your strengths into a brand, while eliminating your weaknesses.
- Make your brand stand out and develop attributes that separate you from the pack.
- Change can come from self-reflection.
- See your big picture, including past, present, and future.
- Build trust through your actions and behaviors.
- There is a high cost of having a bad brand and a great reward for a good one.
- It matters what people think.
- Act with integrity in everything you do.
- You earn the brand that you are or are not.
- Make community service part of how you do business—and you'll get more of it.

Keep learning at: createdemandandstopchasing.com

Chapter 4

Think Like a Pilot: Performance Mindset

"I do not fix problems. I fix my thinking. Then problems fix themselves."

-Louise L. Hay

The morning was cool, and the skies were foggy enough to make a duck think twice about hitting the air.

I'd planned my first "long-distance" solo flight of 50 miles or more to go from Fort Meade to Ocean City, Maryland. Even though I'd only spent 20 student hours in a cockpit—most people need 60+ to get a pilot's license—I was confident I could make that trip.

But nature has its own plans, especially when you're flying.

As I was walking out to do my pre-flight check that morning, the chief flight instructor questioned, "Weather's marginal today, eh?" Which I didn't get, and so, I kept on. In the area I was in, morning fog usually burned off as the sun rose, so it didn't seem like a big deal to me.

Even as a novice, I had soaked up many lessons of the skies. I began applying them both to my flying skills and my new real estate business. The "sharp like a pilot" branding idea had been implemented and was teaching me over a dozen new ways to think strategically and help me form a "performance mindset." You can apply lessons learned from flying to just about anything life throws at you. When I started the ground school portion of flight school, the concepts the instructors taught sounded like they could've come straight out of a Stephen Covey book (think—*The 7 Habits of Highly Effective People*). Only the outcome would be a little heavier: *Implement these concepts, or there's a huge chance you might die*. Nothing like the fear of death to crystalize your thoughts... Given what I'd face later that day, I would need the focus of a thousand Zen masters to survive.

Lessons from the Air

While I prepared for my flight, I put some of my lessons to work. I had learned that human beings perform best according to their own cycles of energy—called *circadian rhythms*. Our bodies have specific and adaptable responses to a 24-hour, light-and-dark cycle. The circadian "clock" controls all facets of our biology, including our brainwaves, level of alertness, blood pressure, and behavior.

Each of our rhythms is different. I've found my rhythm is super sharp in the morning. In my business, I'm totally on top of my game from around 5:00 to 10:00 a.m. This is when I'm most alert. My business has seen major growth every year in part because I use early morning hours to research and work on implementing new aspects of my business.

So, according to my rhythm, I was at the right place at the right time.

Now, I had to plan my flight. There's a saying in the aviation business: The most useless things are the altitude above you, the runway behind you, and the fuel you left in the truck. What this means is you do it the right way instead of the easy way—**no shortcuts**. Like I mentioned earlier, the possibility of death is a *great* motivator. You gain amazing confidence when you know everything you're doing; you are doing right.

After walking around the *Piper Cherokee* and giving it a quick but thorough inside-and-out check, I climbed into the pilot's seat, strapped the visual flight rules **checklist** to my leg, set my radios to the correct frequencies, and asked for clearance to take off.

My checklist inspection showed that my plane was in good shape; its instruments were working, and the radios were operable. Checklists are something pilots use before and during every flight, and for many situations. When you expect your flight to go smoothly, but it doesn't, an emergency checklist puts a plan in place to deal with the unexpected. Flight school emphasizes **emergency procedure planning**, which gives pilots the confidence they can stay calm and work through the drama of an imperfect scenario.

Largely because of the checklist mentality, a pilot might work for 20 years and not make one mistake, something I instantly knew I had to adopt for my real estate life. The compounding effect of doing every single task required for every single project or contract, every single time across a day, week, month and year will make the biggest impact on your life and business.

I'm not the only one to include checklists to improve my business. Several industries have made them a mandatory part of their operations. A physician at Johns Hopkins started a revolution in medicine when he devised a checklist that greatly reduced the number of patients who suffered from hospital-borne infections.

I had fueled up, gone through my checklist, and made sure I was in the best possible shape to fly. I began to **visualize** how my flight would go. To keep myself on top of my game, especially when I face a lot of adversity, I visualize how situations will play out, whether I'm flying or working through a deal.

I encourage the Realtors on my team to visualize every potential mistake or curveball as if they were trying to avoid crashing a plane into a mountain. I want them to make and use a checklist to avoid that crash. Doing so gives them the incentive to understand what can go wrong, to own the situation when it happens, and to work on the intense calm they need to solve the problem.

Missing an inspection repair deadline or forgetting to turn in a client's deposit—or any other real estate "disaster"—can be avoided by developing a crash-into-the-side-of-the-mountain-and-die-if-you-make-a-mistake mentality.

That day, I planned to fly over the Chesapeake Bay and the pancake-flat expanse of Maryland's Eastern Shore, to land at an airstrip in Ocean City, and then fly back to the same small airport between Washington and Baltimore. Once I'd arrived, I was to attend a meeting I couldn't miss with a notable homebuilder. I envisioned smooth sailing once the sun began to peel off the fog and I rose above it.

I communicated with the airport, was cleared, and took off. As a kid with a stutter, it had been important for me to learn to communicate as clearly as possible. Flight school helped me understand the importance of getting your communications exactly right—again, a skill that is essential to a top-flight (no pun intended) real estate transaction.

I powered up to 4,000 feet and looked for my first visual pilot's cue, a river just south of Annapolis. But something was in the air between my plane and the river. The fog wasn't lifting. I couldn't see a thing.

Flying over the bay, it got worse. My next cue—the Bay Bridge—never appeared as the soup surrounding my plane thickened. I could barely see the horizon. But it was there, which gave me a glimmer of hope that I could maintain some visual perspective.

And then I couldn't see the horizon. *Well, shit.*

There I was, 20 hours into my flight-school training, and I was already under "instrument conditions." Without visual cues, I had to depend on dials, gauges, navigation systems, and radios to guide me. Outside of monitoring them, my eyes weren't much use at all. *Was I ready for this? Or was my frickin' branding idea going to get me killed?*

Grace Under Pressure

In flight school, you're taught that when everything goes wrong, you have to manage the situation with serenity and logic.

As it turned out, I was no Zen master, after all. *How could I reach clarity in the middle of fog*?

I kept asking myself, *should I turn back or keep going*? My mind raced to the memory of just a few years earlier, when John F. Kennedy Jr., also a pilot in training, had faced "spatial disorientation" when haze had shrouded the horizon. He made several mistakes that ended up killing himself, his wife, and her sister. And I was next.

When I was younger, I suffered from anxiety attacks. Fortunately, flight school had us work through stress management techniques to cope with taxing situations while in flight. So, instead of wetting my pants in the cockpit, I used relaxation techniques I had learned—which I also instituted into my real estate life from then on.

My mind flooded with recently-learned piloting concepts like putting first things first to aviate, navigate, communicate—which teaches you to prioritize and not let the distraction of navigating and communicating contribute to you crashing your plane. The idea is to focus on the most important tasks first. This concept has been key in business, in understanding how to prioritize, and in helping me to focus on what needs to be done next.

I managed to get across the bay. The GPS indicated I was five minutes outside of Ocean City, but I couldn't see any of the tall resort buildings I had hoped to use as landmarks. Dripping sweat, I radioed in the normal announcement of entering the local air traffic pattern—"Five minutes out, 45-degree angle, downwind," —and then started my approach over the ocean.

As I descended toward the barely visible airstrip, I was overcome with joy. Fortunately, the runway had appeared. I was going to live after all!
But my bout with sheer terror wasn't over. I had forgotten to slow the plane down. I hit the ground at 100 miles per hour, not the 60 mph that would have made for a safer (and smoother) landing. I screamed as the plane

"porpoised" violently down the runway before finally coming to a stop. My heart pounded, but I was alive.

The constant fear of killing myself and my passengers is real. As I revisit it, it forces me to focus on the concepts I discuss in this chapter. If I were ever to feel lost in the skies again, I would remember not to get caught up in maps and the GPS system. *Fly the plane. Carefully figure out the navigation. Take comfort in all the lessons you have learned to bring the risk of death to an acceptable level.*

Treat Your Job as Survival

Even though I was overjoyed that I had lived to tell the tale, I took some time to collect myself before flying back. And I ended up being sore for a whole week from the emotional, mental, and physical stress of wrangling that sucker to the ground. Nevertheless, the ordeal confirmed the importance of incorporating many of my lessons from flight school into a new way of thinking, a performance mindset that allows me to approach, focus, and manage work with the same thought processes a pilot uses to make it home safely every day.

Cultivating that sharp like a pilot approach has proven indispensable. It makes me view each type of task differently, with more purpose, focus, and better decision-making.

Most real estate agents aren't taught much about mindset. We're taught to do all sorts of stuff, but I never saw much training about mindset like I did in flight school. It was a crucial learning experience that helped me implement 110% effort.

Pilot training infused me with adaptability, flexibility, and urgency to get through difficult and unforeseen situations.

My would-be "disaster in the sky" taught me the importance of top performance—the planning, the dedication, and the need to think about doing a job *as if your life depends on it.*

Obviously, my performance in the air that day wasn't exactly my best. I misunderstood what the flight instructor on duty meant by "marginal" weather. I didn't ask him to clarify, which means I could have listened—

communicated—better. I missed my opportunity to *fly or not fly* which is a logical process where a pilot considers all factors, including the weather, to determine if the flight should be made. Because I had visualized clear sailing, I didn't factor in the foggy scenario, but I needed to be aware of it to survive. They should rename the saying *die or not die*, because it forces you to make better decisions, and compounded across time, will help your life and business soar.

Later on, as I neared the end of my 60 hours of student flying time, I realized that my instructor had yet to teach me two of the trickiest maneuvers: stalls and 360-degree turns at a 45-degree angle without losing altitude. Inconveniently, that realization came the night before my "check ride," which is the final exam in the air to earn a pilot's license.

I'd have to learn these two tricks and pass my test on the same day.

That morning, my instructor and I went through those final lessons and then came back to rest a bit before making my pivotal flight with the tester. Later, as I walked back out to the tarmac in 95-degree weather, I realized I wasn't the same screaming guy who'd "porpoised" my way down the runway several weeks before.

The student who had tested before me walked back toward the airport in the opposite direction. He was hangdog. He had failed by landing on the wrong runway, yikes! Despite witnessing that setback along with the 95-degree heat, I felt a refreshing chill. It was a strong sensation; I knew there was no way I could blow it. My mindset was untouchable. I was going to perform confidently and calmly. I aced the tests, even with what I had learned that morning.

Since then, I've maintained that high-performing attitude, a mindset that has served me very well, even when my altitude is zero.

This new approach added to my brand.

Not only am I a pilot who is maintaining the appearance and reputation of being sharp like a pilot, but I have a new performance outlook that makes my work better, and my clients appreciate me even more. It's one thing to believe you've changed your mindset; it's another to actually have earned solid accomplishments, like acing flight school. Earlier I mentioned Dweck's now famous book, *Mindset: The New Science of Success.* She makes the distinction between a fixed mindset, in which you believe there's no more room for personal growth, and a growth mindset, which implies we grow by challenging ourselves, which leads to success.

Growth experiences can be gained in every area of life. Despite that terror-inducing solo flight, I used what I had been taught to keep me calm, cool, and collected...what I didn't know how to do before flying lessons. I had to execute the procedures correctly and completely every single time, make better decisions every single time, and put first things first every single time. Learning to fly gave me an amazing performance mindset. If I could master the potentially lethal and dangerous art of flying a plane, I could handle learning a lot about life and business in the process.

Trying to give this business 110% without the correct mindset to implement that effort, is like trying to solo on your first day of flight school. It won't work.

You don't necessarily need flying lessons to implement a performance mindset, although it wouldn't hurt. But you should treat your business like it's your life. Because it probably is.

RON'S RULES FROM THE COCKPIT:

- Treat everything like your life depends on it to get real results.
- Learn your circadian rhythm and optimize your work times around it.
- Have a checklist mentality: Do tasks correctly and completely every single time.
- Visualize your successful day and plan to bring the calm wherever it is needed.
- Stop taking shortcuts. They will kill you or your business.
- Be prepared to deal with the unexpected.

- A performance mindset will help you perform at your best and communicate better.
- Learn to manage your stress with relaxation techniques.
- Think sharp like a pilot and your business will soar.
- Learn to prioritize and not let distractions get you off course.

Keep learning at: createdemandandstopchasing.com

Chapter 5

Relationship-Building Science

"Mental triggers are things that influence our actions on a very fundamental level all day long, each and every day. When used together, their impact is compounded."

-Jeff Walker

The offer caught my eye.

A new tech company had developed a brand new "lead generating technology" that, according to the sales rep, combined more than 100 real estate data points to create a newfangled algorithm. Their new product was "guaranteed" to increase my sales volume and identify leads by predicting prospects that would soon want to be in the market. According to the rep, this exciting new tool had already helped top agents around the country lock down their territory.

The company even made ordering seamless. Though the service was absurdly expensive, the sales rep said he could do me a favor and give me a large discount, making the tool a tad less pricey—if I acted on their offer *now*. If I didn't, I was told, one of my competitors certainly would. And if they did, they'd have the drop on me. They would gain the technology and the added business that I would "lose" by not buying in.

What could I do? Feeling simultaneously fascinated, enticed, envious, and pressured, I took their "discounted" offer.

After spending a considerable chunk of change, I came to realize I'd been "triggered" to buy a service I didn't need. And that "amazing" product might work for some, but barely moved the needle on my sales meter.

That "new lead generating technology" may not have worked for me, but the sales pitch certainly did. It pulled subconscious strings in my mind, triggering mental cues that we all respond to. The company had sold me by messing with my head, which happens to all of us.

As real estate agents, we're enticed to buy a range of trainings, new technologies, and leads all the time. Every year, there's a shiny new object that beckons us, tapping into the anxiety and vulnerability we feel about getting new business. We're regularly "triggered" to open our wallets for products and services that, ultimately, don't do much for us.

This is the salesy side of mental triggers—used effectively they can trigger you to buy something whether you need it or not.

Triggers are powerful, and that's why sales and marketing companies have included them in their approaches for many years. But there's a decent way to use them that doesn't involve trickery, deception, or outright manipulation. If you use your understanding of how they work, the reward will come in the form of many more people who choose to hire you.

Don't Sell—Connect

Your understanding of how triggers work can be used as an alternate way to encourage people to hire you without using sales pitches or scripts. Nothing about my use of triggers represents a conscious effort to sell. It might seem hard to believe, but people will work with you even if you don't pitch to them or memorize a meticulously worded script. It's about going deeper than that surface level connection, to become what most people will subconsciously be attracted to.

Since I wasn't going to hustle after people and pitch to them, I needed to learn how and why they'd behaved the way they did. I investigated everything I could find about influence and connection, and the practice of stacking mental triggers was fascinating.

It's Science

There's a science behind the concept of influence. Robert Cialdini, one of the leaders in influence research, has shown several major influences that motivate people to take action.

In his bestselling book, *Influence: The Psychology of Persuasion*, Cialdini reports how mother turkeys are automatically triggered to coddle and nurture chicks that speak up with a "cheep-cheep," but ignore and perhaps even kill those that don't. Their trigger reflex is so strong, in fact, they will care for a stuffed version of one of their predators, the polecat, if it's outfitted with a pre-recorded "cheep-cheep" tape.

These triggers, called "fixed-action patterns," play out consistently in nature. They are basically automatic responses.

What does the animal kingdom have to do with us? We're obviously creatures of reason and consideration—well, most of the time—and we don't just predictably react to stimuli like bird brains do, right? Or, do we?

Cialdini adds that when salespeople notice triggers, they can become their "weapons of influence." The exact reason being that people have fixed-action patterns similar to animals that we can tap into. Everyone has their own "preprogrammed tapes" that guide our behavior under certain circumstances.

Getting to know the contents of those tapes—aka triggers—can help you understand the most effective way that people make subconscious decisions. As you improve, you'll learn how to keep the best triggers in mind, and how to use them correctly. The more ways you can trigger people correctly, the more likely it is you're going to get their business...

If you can give people the feeling that they can like and trust you, even though they don't have a scrap of information at their disposal, then they'll be more likely to work with you.

Without the help of triggers, Cialdini adds, "We would stand frozen— cataloging, appraising, and calibrating— as the time for action sped by and away."

Stacking Them Up

Even those of us who are hip to the "weapons" can fall prey to triggering. Witness my experience with the lead gen tech company. It used several scientifically proven types of triggers to hook me, and then reel me in:

The "Weapons":

Authority. Triggering feelings of authority in the subconscious of your customer means they will see you as an expert in your field. The tech company's algorithm used facts (putting together more than 100 data points!) to make it appear as if it had become the instant authority on the new technology. Authority is a super trigger; it makes it easy for us to make decisions because we are programmed to obey those in an authority position.

Reciprocity. People feel obligated to give back to those who are seen as doing something for them. That company's product carried a five-figure price tag that wasn't for the sheepish. But to show me they appreciated my wallet, similar to what a car salesman might do when trying to sell to you, they shaved off a few thousand dollars, creating the feeling of reciprocity. This kind of feeling emanates from the basic idea, "you do something for me (give me a discount), and I'll feel like I should do something for you (buy your system)." Car salespeople know the feeling of reciprocity is so strong, they use it masterfully in making it easy for you to pay them back, by buying a car. That's at the core of the concept of reciprocity, and it exists outside of the sales arena. It's the feeling you should buy someone a beer because they bought you one. Reciprocity is a super trigger.

Social proof. The sales rep ensured me there were top agents around the country who had locked down their territory before others because they'd bought in. In doing this, they were tapping social proof, which is a trigger that is tripped when we do something we see others doing. If we see that other people are paying good money for an item—or even if we're just told that they have paid good money—we're more likely to buy. "Usually, when a lot of people are doing something," Cialdini writes, "it is the right thing to do." But not always—as I unfortunately learned.

Scarcity. We're more likely to want what we can get *now* if we're told we won't be able to get it in the future. By telling customers to "Act now!" with a warning that they'll miss out if they don't, you trigger their fear of being left behind. Scarcity works because of what Cialdini calls "anticipated regret." We think about the future and see ourselves ruing an action not taken. When the sales rep told me that one of my competitors would likely buy the technology and gain business instead of me, I experienced anticipated regret, and I signed on.

Using Triggers, the Right Way

Authority, reciprocity, social proof, and scarcity are exceptionally strong triggers that marketers and others have come to understand and use regularly. But that's not all; there are a half dozen more triggers that need to be understood. But it's important to know how to use them. I don't use triggers to sell people; I use my understanding of how they work to help mold the person I am.

If you understand the way someone's subconscious can be triggered, you'll understand you've actually been selling all along.

As it pertains to scarcity, it's known that smothering people with attention causes them to run from us. If you understand the trigger principle of scarcity, however, you won't smother. You'll "touch" people much less, and if you make those touches good, you might even create **anticipation**, another strong trigger. People will anticipate you more if you are less available.

Social proof means building a strong reputation, getting great online reviews, gaining knowledge of the market, having a regular community presence, utilizing smart social media, and earning top-ranked sales figures to create **authority** in the minds of many in the community. Dressing the part doesn't hurt, either...

Reciprocity is a simple concept: Give to people, and they will give something back. I initially got involved in the community for branding purposes, not realizing the force of reciprocity and how much business it would bring me. You can't expect business out of doing good, but I'd be lying if I told you it hadn't generated a lot of business for me. I give my time, interest, and money to a lot of causes, and take reciprocity to the community level by serving with many nonprofits, sponsoring amazing events, and throwing great parties. I serve because it makes me feel good, but the reward of business isn't so bad either. In a nutshell, I'd rather do good in the community than cold call and chase people. As a top-producing agent in Baltimore, I'd argue it's a better use of my time all the way around.

Another powerful trigger that takes time to cultivate with others is **trust**. If you want someone to hire you, or be influenced by you, it's much easier if they have confidence in you. I build all my relationships on trust, by always doing what I say. My behavior is predictable. In doing so, people appreciate you long after a deal is done—and are much more likely to do business with you later.

Our massive effort in creating a hardworking, sharp, community-service-oriented brand, and hiring great agents affects our **likeability**, another strong trigger. People hire people they like. Add as many positive traits as you can and drop the negative ones we shared in chapter 3. Work on being more likable.

We sponsor over a dozen citywide events a year because we like to provide a fun time for the city and the neighborhoods where we work (thankfully, it creates **reciprocity**). We invite all our prospects, clients, and friends, creating a **community** that **anticipates** the **ritual** of our events. Become known for throwing great events, and they can become rituals. The ritual and community triggers are strong and pull people together in a powerful way. Throwing great events (rituals) is an effective way to build a community full of fun people that many others will want to belong to. People love to be part of something bigger than themselves. Church and NFL game days are powerful examples of rituals that build a community.

The presence of other people at those events, meanwhile, invokes **social proof**, the idea that people will be more likely to buy or take part in something when others do. My team benefits from social proof, too. Our glowing reviews on Zillow and other sites create a heightened appeal triggering others to use us.

The way triggers work is simple but powerful, and marketers use them masterfully when convincing your subconscious to buy something. They stack them up until you feel compelled to make the purchase. When the feeling to purchase something becomes overwhelming, that's when you know a marketer has stacked a bunch of triggers on you. A few days later when you've thought your purchase through a bit more concisely, you think, *why did I buy that yellow fanny pack?* It's ironic. The game-changing tactic every Realtor needs to know: how to trigger the subconscious, is used on them regularly by marketers selling technology, training, or leads that end up not being what you anticipated. The game-changing magic you need is used on you every day.

If you have ever sold to big corporations, you are trained to call on the top decision makers—which in a lot of cases is the CEO. But, first, you have to get through their executive assistant (aka the gatekeeper) who screens all the sales calls. If there were a way to get around the gatekeeper and go directly to the decision maker, you would take it. As a realtor I compare someone's subconscious to their "decision maker" and their conscious to their "gatekeeper." Why would you want to tangle with their gatekeeper with scripted and manipulative closing routines when you can communicate directly with their decision-making subconscious?

The most important takeaway is knowing how to understand and use triggers to help you form and present the best version of yourself. Make yourself into someone most people will want to hire. Making that subconscious connection on many different levels will help your business big time.

RON'S RULES FOR THE JEDI-IN-TRAINING:

The Triggers:

- Authority – People are preprogrammed to accept those in an authority position. Become an authority.
- Reciprocity – The automatic feeling to do something for someone if they've done something for you. Do as much as you can for others.
- Scarcity – When there is less of something available we will want it more. Stop smothering and find the right balance to make people want more of you.
- Anticipation – The expectation of being rewarded. Make yourself less available, and you will be better received.
- Likeability – Listen, be honest and take care of those around you. Work on being more likable.
- Social proof – When uncertain, we take cues from other people. Make sure you have good social proof.

- Community – People like the sense of belonging to a community, whether online or in real life. Build a community of good people and others will want to be part of it.
- Rituals – People love to gather with their friends, think church, Monday night football, etc. Throw great events.
- Trust – Do what you say. When people trust you, they turn to you for help, business, and advice.

Don't use triggers to manipulate, but to understand how to make a direct connection with others' subconscious decision-making.

Sign up for free instant access to our Relationship-Building Science module, part of our Create Demand and Stop Chasing Business online course at: relationshipbuildingscience.com. Learn more about connecting with the real decision maker, the subconscious.

Chapter 6

Friends Not Funnels: Authentic Sphere-Building

"When someone shows you who they are, believe them the first time."
-Maya Angelou

When I first launched my business, I realized I had to focus on creating the best version of myself in every aspect. It took a massive effort to develop my branding ideas but becoming *sharp like a pilot* led to having a performance mindset. If I wanted the chance to compete with agents who were highly involved in the community, I would have to get involved as much as I could with whoever I could.

The first thing I did was join an events committee for a nonprofit where we planned four fundraising events that year. After a few successful events, it hit me—*I truly enjoy helping people*. Surrounding myself with the committee members and those involved with the nonprofit was very rewarding; they were the type of people I wanted to become.

As I became more and more engaged with community-oriented people, I transitioned from merely trying to fix my brand to be competitive, to being someone who sincerely believed in the causes I took part in. No selling…just helping. Although, it did start to lead to a few calls here and there.

"Hey, Ron, can you come over? I want to sell my house."

"Hey, Ron, my nephew is moving to Baltimore. Can you help him buy a place?"

"Hey, Ron…my agent is going to *kill* me, but I'm thankful you're helping with the park."

"Hey Ron, I know five other agents, but I'd like to work with you. Thank you for all you do."

As much as my team and I enjoy the reciprocity of new clients, it's still our focus to be major contributors to the communities around us. I do good for people, and it's great that others see me as someone they want to do business with, too.

Expand Your Circle

Now that you've created the best version of yourself, put into place a winning mindset, and have a better understanding of how you affect others, you'll need new ways to meet people worthy of your time, so that you can grow your sphere of influence.

I've created a simple three-step process, which I call the "friends not funnels" approach, which allows me to meet a lot of new people without throwing them down a sales funnel. Instead, I build sincere relationships. The reward is finding that people will appreciate your sincerity and honest kindness, and it will come back to you tenfold:

Service. Serve your community. Originally, getting involved with the community was an idea to improve my brand, and it did just that—helping others became part of who I am. And it uncovered a passion for community service, which led me to get involved with as many nonprofit groups as I can handle. I never expect reciprocity, but it tends to happen when you sincerely give your time and energy to people and their causes. I hear it all the time, "[Another Realtor I know] will hate me, but I'm going to use you because of all the work you do in my neighborhood." Giving back has become such an integral part of my life, I encourage all my associates to do so as well. It's an enjoyable way to support others and meet more community-minded people in the process.

Social.

Throw high-quality events for the community, and they will appreciate you. Each year, I bring everyone together to throw at least three big parties and sponsor notable events that draw crowds of thousands. We invite all the new people we meet each year to our events and bring them into our welcoming community of friends and clients. These events are anticipated, have become rituals, build community and social proof, generate reciprocity, and make us more likable—so, we hit a full range of triggers. When we "touch" you with an invite, there's a better chance it's going to impact you than a pumpkin pie recipe card would. For those of you like me, who did a lot of partying back in the day, this is where your party organizing skills can help you.

Go a Little Deeper. Popular concert series attracting thousands of people and other events with hundreds of people in attendance aren't just shallow attempts to drink. At these parties and events, you get to spend time with and get to know people better. I set later dates for lunch, breakfast, or drinks with the people I meet, so, I can get to know them better one on one. I love getting to know new people, and you can't truly connect with people if your main objective is putting them in a sales funnel. You must have a sincere interest in relationships, and the business will follow.

Some other ideas include coaching a sport with your kids (kickball, football, etc.), attending a book club, getting involved with a business organization, and setting up an account on MeetUp (meetup.com). Meeting people doesn't have to be complicated. Start conversations with people around you, walk your dog, host dinner parties and invite new guests, join a gym, take any class you want like dance or improv, find a church or religious community, work from a coffee shop, eat dinner at the bar in a nice restaurant…and the list goes on.

A Better Way to Find People

Before I began consciously growing my network, my sphere included roughly 250 people. Now it's more than 1,400 and growing. I've been on five nonprofit boards. I want to be generous with everybody, knowing that it will benefit both them and me, for now, and in the long run.

I tip 30 percent at restaurants, help people when they ask, and spend a lot of time out in public behaving myself. I don't tell off-color jokes or engage in angry discussions. And, although this may sound like cheap advice, *it's important to try and be a good friend to the people you spend time with.* Really listen to what they have to say.

I allow people to talk about what they want. They're the ones who bring up real estate—not me. I'm just there to connect with them, one human being to another. I manifest sincere interest in the relationship.

Because of the "friends not funnels" approach, I've created an alternative model to the same-old, same-old—doing business door-knocking, prospecting, making cold calls or harassing friends for work. It's a genuine approach that helps you grow your business without making a sales pitch.

The *friends not funnels* concept has been crucial in elevating my team as a leader in Baltimore's business community. I can guarantee that putting sincere effort into relationships, not sales funnels, will change the way people see you and put you in a position as a go-to Realtor.

If you're doing everything right in this regard (including following the process above), your phone will be ringing off the hook—and it will keep ringing.

There are other advantages to the *friends not funnels* strategy. It will help you become a better person. It will improve the image of the real estate industry. You'll draw solid agents to your team. And you'll be the envy of other Realtors who will wonder how you've managed to pull off such impressive sales growth, year after year.

I've replaced cold-calling, prospecting, and door-knocking with doing community service. If you enjoy helping people and have a sincere interest in connecting with like-minded folks, there is no better way to expand your circle.

Great Ideas to Meet People and Do Good in Your Community

- Join a fundraising committee for a local nonprofit
- Join an event-organizing committee for a local nonprofit
- Join a board of a local nonprofit
- Volunteer at a Ronald McDonald House or if you are in my area, consider Believe in Tomorrow
- Help organize a community blood drive
- Organize a team and participate in a charity race
- Volunteer to help at a charity event
- Organize a team and do a charity race or ride
- Sponsor neighborhood events—we're a big fan of concerts in the park
- Organize a toy drive for Toys for Tots
- Volunteer at a local homeless shelter

- Coach a youth sports team
- Organize an Easter egg hunt for kids in a homeless shelter
- Volunteer at a senior center
- Organize a Bingo night for nursing home residents
- Sponsor a holiday for senior citizens
- Volunteer at an animal shelter
- Volunteer at your local park
- Organize/participate in a trail work program at your local park/trail system
- Organize/participate in the cleanup of a local waterway
- Help build a house with Habitat for Humanity
- Help repair a local homeless shelter
- Volunteer as a Big Brother, or Sister
- Organize a winter clothes drive to collect jackets, scarves, and gloves to be donated
- Volunteer at a police station, firehouse, or hospital
- Join or start a neighborhood watch program
- Raise money to install new playground equipment for your neighborhood park

- Organize a fundraiser and raise funds to repair a run-down playground
- Volunteer to clean up trash at a community event
- Organize a neighborhood clean-up after a big storm

*List inspiration from PrepScholar.

The idea is to do good in the community and meet more people. Focus on building meaningful relationships and use your understanding of triggers to help you become better at presenting the best version of yourself.

RON'S RULES FOR THE CONVERTED SOCIALITE:

- Use the "friends not funnels" approach as a successful method for growing a network of people who will naturally want to work with you.
- Make community service part of how you do business—and you'll get more of it.
- Helping people helps you become a better person, and your business become a better business.
- Elevate your standing and our industry with great "service and social" events in the community.

Keep learning at: createdemandandstopchasing.com

Chapter 7

Fix Your Feed

"We don't have a choice on whether we do social media, the question is how well we do it."
-Erik Qualman

Last New Year's, I was in Waikiki visiting family with Jeni, my lovely fiancée (who is now my wife). We had just gotten back from a catamaran cruise around Diamond Head and wanted to find a nice, sandy spot on the crowded beach to bake in the sun.

As we scanned the endless sea of people in search for some space, a super jolly fellow shouted over, said hello, and made room for us to spread out our beach towels. We got situated as our new friend seemed to work the crowd, talking with everyone around him. He was very engaging, super likable. I already felt like I owed him something—he had triggered my reciprocity response for helping us out.

I'm thinking, he's *got* to be a sales guy, so I asked him what he sells. Surprisingly, he told me he'd been practicing medicine for 27 years as an ER doctor in Newport Beach, California. The way he emphasized "practicing" struck me as odd. *Practicing*? *For all those years*?

But he *had* used the right word: "Every day, for the past 27 years when I go to work, everything is always changing. And I learn something new. It humbles me, but I continue to learn—and *practice* medicine."

In a world, where too many people are happy to flout big egos and can't help but brag about their successes, the doctor's outlook about his work was refreshing. Coincidentally, I was scrolling through Facebook on my phone at the time and saw some of the most ridiculous posts I'd seen all day. This is probably the ONLY time I would ever compare medicine to social media, but—like medicine, social media is a practice. It's always changing, and *we* are always *learning*, always practicing.

This notion of *practicing* resonated with me. We are all a work in progress when it comes to learning new technology; that's why my team and I make sure to stay on top of best practices when it comes to social media. Our profiles and business pages are treated as an extension of who we are. It is critical to put enough thought into your posts to entice interaction, or you can lose a ton of business. That's like losing patients on the operating table. If you lost enough of them, who would trust you to be their surgeon?

Dos and Don'ts of Social Media Posts

Your personal profiles should be an extension of what you do in real life: making connections and building better relationships...and sharing pics of your dogs, of course. Conversely, you should minimize the damage you do. It's important to remember that social media is dangerous, and it can dramatically affect your chances of people wanting to hire you. Here's what you should incorporate into your posts and what you should avoid at all costs:

Do...

Ask yourself this first, as I do before I put anything out on my newsfeed" *"What does this post trigger?"*

Establish Authority. Make these posts scarce and modest, no more than once a month. Posting photos of you winning a sales award, or suited up with clients, or sharing a great online review can help establish authority. And authority is even better established when others share what a great person you are rather than when you share your awesomeness. Our business page and our promoted posts do more of the authority work.

Create Reciprocity. Sponsoring an event, giving back to the community, promoting a fundraiser, volunteering at the senior center, or just about anything where you're helping people will work. People who share the same interests will want to reciprocate.

Make Scarcity Work. People will look forward to seeing your posts if you post in moderation. Less is more in this case. If you smother people with constant updates, you will chase them away.

Establish Anticipation. Post too much, and you are a bother. Post in moderation and people will anticipate hearing from you. Try to get some nice pictures on your page every once in a while. I get a lot of likes when I post beautiful photos of the woods from my mountain biking trips or the snowcapped slopes when I snowboard. True beauty is rare, which triggers the scarcity principle.

Encourage Likeability. Be personable, authentic, fair, and honest. Don't be mean or a know-it-all. If you're posting a comment, figure out the vibe of what's going on before you chime in.

Use Social Proof. The best form of social proof happens when others review or comment about you on social media. Share a new online review (no more than twice a month), or photos of a crowded fundraiser or client appreciation party you threw. People like to follow the crowd.

Start Rituals. Throw or sponsor great events that people look forward to and share the invites on social media.

Establish Community. Luckily, Facebook makes it easier to take part in the communities you want to become involved in through their Facebook groups or event creation. Whether you create your own group or event to find other dog parents or join an existing one, there are countless options to find the right people you want to have in your circle. Establishing community ties in directly with starting rituals as well. From the event you threw (that was highly anticipated), you can share photos and videos to your Facebook group. This reinforces your community and allows you to keep expanding it. Communities are built around events, new clients, past clients, existing friends, and new friends. Sharing memories of your events with your circle creates the feeling of community.

Create Trust. Make sure you follow through on your online promises, whether you sign up for that 5K or you hit "Yes" to attend a friend's event. Show up, or you lose that trust.

Use Novelty. Novelty can be achieved by creating fun posts. Cool science stories, obscure factoids, great writers—all can be a part of creating novelty. Be careful, though: What might be novel to you could be weird or even creepy to others.

Be Authentic. Share the curveballs we all get in life. Don't try to be perfect. But be careful not to turn people off. Authenticity is important but sharing that time you blacked out at the bar won't trigger any warm and fuzzy feelings.

Give People More "Love" and More Dogs. I got over 800 likes when I posted about my wedding engagement and hundreds of likes from photos of my dog. Make these personal pieces of your life scarce, and only post them if they are interesting. If your dog is as photogenic as mine, take the time to choose one out of your daily canine photo shoot.

Don't...

Be Purposely Vague. This is what we call *vaguebooking,* meaning someone posts a loaded phrase or question as their status, without explanation. Don't be that person who mysteriously posts something and expects others to ask what's wrong.

Become a "Wall Hog." Don't be the girl in a bikini or the guy taking selfies at the gym who posts "positivity" 26 times a day hoping to accumulate likes while taking over our newsfeed. Being a *Wall Hog* works against the mental triggers you are trying to stack up online. Instead, create scarcity to make people anticipate your posts. If you're posting over a few times a day, it's too much. If you feel like you've posted too much, take a few days off. Don't smother people—it chases them away. Establishing social proof doesn't mean posting ten times per day. If you are not offering value and posting memorable content, you come across as insecure and not well-balanced (because you seem to want/need likes for some personal reason).

Over Self-Promote. Personal status holds no rank on social media and should hold no weight when it comes to your posts. Nobody gives a shit what kind of car you drive, or how much you made last year. Bombard your followers with pictures of your car, your big house, or how great you and your kids are, and they will tune you out, if not resent you. This is the opposite way to achieve authority and likeability. Remember these two triggers are based on your positioning of yourself and your brand as *knowing* what you are talking about in your industry. It's also true that people *want* to like you, as much as it is true that over-promotion and appearing to brag will ensure people will have a hard time liking you.

Aim to Go Viral. Stick to the triggers and connect with the subconscious. Did you know 99 times out of 100 you will fail and will fall on deaf ears? They call it 15 minutes of fame for a reason. Except now, it's more like 15 blinks before the person you are trying to engage scrolls down to the next distraction.

Overdo It on the Business Posts on Your Personal Profile. Know your limit and share news of an open house or a new development, but without being too salesy. Social media is all about sounding casual. Make your post interesting and inspiring without making the reader feel like they're being sold to. Strike a balance between actually giving a shit about your business, but not trying too hard to show it. There is a reason your personal and business pages are separate, but you are in a field that does overlap into personal branding, so yes, you do want to share what you are up to business-wise on your personal page. Still, your page is where people come to get to know you and interact with you on a deeper level. They expect to learn about your personal life, and cats, etc., while also hearing periodically about how business is going.

Chase Likes. We all have an urge to share a breaking news story, but you're better off letting everyone else take care of it. There's no need to repost the latest political debacle or celebrity scandal and smother people with the same news they've been hammered with 50 times already. Sharing this type of drivel is the equivalent of executing anti-authority.

Even Think About Politics, Religion or Sex. Don't go there unless you're ready to turn off a high percentage of your friends. This last election split the country down the middle, and both sides are crazy in their passions. Realtors who take the bait and post for or against a candidate, are what I call *halfers.* They instantly turn off a huge percentage of their social circle, thereby losing a lot of potential business. Look no further if you want to achieve the opposite of every single trigger listed.

When It Comes to your Business Page...

You certainly want to use the same rules you use for your personal profile on your business page, but we're going to focus heavily on capturing leads with our business pages.

This is the part that is always changing; it seems like every six months there is a new way to capture leads from social media. We could write a whole book on this topic alone, but it would be outdated in a few months.

At the writing of this book, just about everything we are doing is going to video. Video home tours, market reports, seller and buyer tips, etc. We call them sticky videos because they all drive traffic to a capture page where visitors register and become a lead in our system. Our website company Real Geeks has a great Facebook tool that allows us to create a range of posts that drive traffic back to our site where we capture it.

We spend $1,000-2,000 a month on Facebook advertising, constantly changing our approach until we find ads that work. Our cost per lead fluctuates between $2-30.

Instead of writing a whole book on this topic our goal was to create a community of agents who would share their business posts that work with our Facebook group at facebook.com/createdemandstopchasing.

Just like my ER doctor friend in Waikiki, I'm still "practicing" social media every day. For lead gen, capture, and my own personal use, my methods are always changing, and I'm constantly learning. Just remember, your posts affect people subconsciously, whether you stack positive mental triggers or carelessly put up a humble brag about your paycheck. It's up to you, to use your social media *to help or hurt you.*

RON'S RULES FOR THE NEWSFEED:

- Before you publish that post, ask yourself if it triggers authority, reciprocity, social proof, community, rituals, likeability, trust, scarcity, and anticipation.
- Don't be a wall hog.

- Continue to practice.

Keep learning at: createdemandandstopchasing.com

Chapter 8

Full Throttle

"There are no secrets to success. It is the result of preparation, hard work, and learning from failure."
-Colin Powell

Taking off Fast

When I started rebranding myself, I had already created a new me. I had a new mindset. I was working on better ways to connect and get involved in the community. Social media wasn't around yet. It came a few years later.

My simple idea of going full throttle was to reconnect with every single person I knew. I had disappeared for a bit, made a ton of changes, and was ready to reconnect, with a focus on building better relationships.

In 2004, (pre-Facebook) I had 250 people in my sphere of influence. I knew them well enough to call and touch base with them.

I started my day at 6 a.m., and I'd go to the office and create a list of 5-20 people who I was calling that day. I'd plan out my day, and when it got to a reasonable hour, I would make my calls.

When you disappear for a bit and make a ton of changes in your life, people want to hear about it. Four out of five people I reached out to suggested we catch up for lunch, coffee or drinks. I didn't have to pitch them; they pitched me! This was simply reconnecting and catching up with friends, no selling, no pitching, no scripts; I truly had a sincere interest in being a better friend.

Every single call went like this:

Me: "Hey, Tom, how's it going, bud?"

Tom: "Dude, where ya been hiding?"

Me: "Just been slammed with real estate and flight school."

Tom: "What? Flight school. What are you talking about?"

Me: "Yeah, I've been so busy! I go in around 6 a.m., get some work done, then run off to flight school for a couple hours..."

People I knew were so interested to hear about all my changes, and at the end of those calls, it became clear that I had become hard-working, was sharp enough to fly a plane and was interested in reconnecting and being a better friend.

I made about 250 calls in three weeks, and those calls generated ten contracts in my third month. Also, those first 250 calls started me on my path to be a better friend and earning a lot more business. I didn't need leads. My brand was good; my work ethic was good; my skill level was good. I wasn't a pain-in-the-ass sales guy, and I made a concerted effort to care more about the people I knew. I became a go-to Realtor in a lot of people's minds and have worked to stay that way ever since.

After becoming a better me, my launch was simply calling and reconnecting with everyone I knew, and it worked amazingly well. It's fairly simple; you just have to do it.

Getting a handful of deals done with people you know will make it so much easier when you start doing deals with new leads or people you have just met. This is especially true if you are new to real estate and don't have any or much experience with helping people buy or sell a home. After all, this is the service you are going to market and promote big time. Understanding how to do it before working with strangers will make it a heck of a lot easier on you.

Patience

Learn your Realtor craft before you go overboard promoting yourself on social media or elsewhere. When you are brand new, you have a lot to learn, and you're not quite ready for the full marketing blitz...yet. Once you get some deals under your belt and develop a good understanding of what you're doing, then it's a good time to launch and promote your business in a big way.

Unbalance

As a small business person, you will have to live an unbalanced life. From putting massive effort into your brand to starting your day early, to doing whatever you need to do to generate revenue. The idea of a 9 to 5 job should be a distant memory. Plan for some long days if you're going to break away from the crowd.

I always think of my job like a baseball season. October to December is like winter training, and I'm working on all the new ideas I've found throughout the year, trying to figure what we are going to do differently this upcoming year. My workdays get longer (10+ hours, six days a week) when most agents take it easy that time of year. January through February is spring training, and I'm working around the clock (12-hour days, six days a week) to set up that season. March, April, May, and June are our summer season, and I'm working around the clock (12-hour days, six days a week). Late June through August (fall), our market slows a bit, and you can catch a breather (8-hour days, five days a week) and get off the throttle a bit. September is my recovery month for the whole year, and I can take it easy and rest my mind before I start the whole cycle again in October.

Half the year I get up around 5 a.m. and hit the gym so I can connect with my early-morning health nut friends, the other half I get up at 7 a.m. so I can connect with my late-night friends.

Every Day I Say to Myself

"I know the work I'm doing today was better than yesterday and regardless of any problems will make my tomorrow even better. I don't have time to sit around and talk about the good ol' days; I'm making those days today. I'm going to hustle, learn, implement, and repeat. I'm going to bring the calm and not the chaos. I don't create issues; I solve them. My success won't be casual. I love the grind and embrace the process. I have no time for hope. I'll be the first one in, and the last one out and I'm going to make some shit happen today!"

Tightening the Screws

If you hit the ground running like I did with a lot of transactions in my first few months, you might get so busy that it will take you years to go back and set up your business in the best way possible. We will all have different variables in how we set up, but there are some aspects of our business that are universal to all of us. My business operation is scalable, efficient, and cost-effective. I make my new team members set up properly right out of the gate before they get busy. Doing the same will save you thousands if not tens of thousands of dollars—guaranteed.

You are a small business. You will wear about 10 hats when you start. As you get busier, you will quickly hire people to handle some of those hats. Here are the top things you will need to get on top of ASAP. Many fail at this business in the first three to six months. Don't make the same mistakes.

Learn This Business

You can make big commissions in this business, but it will take hard work and a lot of learning. Become a sponge and learn as much as you can. It's easy to find the top selling books for Realtors on Amazon, and there are so many great videos and podcasts from top producers as well. Check out keepingitreal.com and hibandigital.com for helpful videos and podcasts from top Realtors explaining what they do to be successful. I took every designation course I could get my hands on as soon as I could. And I got my GRI and ABR. Within a couple of years, I had nine designations. Always be learning = Make more money!

Pick the Right Office

You must decide what brokerage to affiliate with. Every brokerage is going to have its pros and cons, and you should look at many before you choose. Figure out what is important to you, training, location, commission splits, etc. The bottom line for me was simple and all about business. When the consumer hires a realtor, nowadays they don't give a lot of value to working with the brokerage. They choose to work with the broker because they feel they can trust them. I remember reading that when a consumer makes a decision to work with a realtor, less than 5% of their choice has to do with their association with the brokerage. Lead-generating sites like Zillow, Trulia and realtor.com have stripped the lead generating activities from most brokerages. I feel more affiliated with Zillow sometimes than I do with my brokerage. My bottom-line brokerage selection is this: With the money you are taking from my commission what am I getting in return? Could I spend this money better and get a more direct impact for me? If you're giving a brokerage 30% a year and you make $100K in commission, they take $30K. Figure out if your split is worth it. Did you get leads and support that made up for it?

Team or No Team

I started on an eight-person team because it seemed like a great way to get off the ground. Unfortunately, in my case, I was the low man on the totem pole and didn't get many team leads. Fortunately, I didn't need the leads because what I was doing was working so well. After six months 95% of my business was self-generated, and I needed help with the self-gen stuff as it was becoming more than I could handle. So, I left the team and established my own. Working on a team can be an excellent way to make a living, as long as the team has your best interests at heart.

Your Business Entity

The way you set up your business entity will help separate your personal and business finances. A lot of agents start as a sole proprietor and comingle all their business and personal expenses. When you ramp up and do well, this will become a nightmare that you will spend way too much time tracking. In most cases, setting up as an LLC will make the most sense and will allow you to keep your banking separate. Check with an accountant. It is not expensive or difficult to set up an LLC and have your brokerage pay the LLC. When you earn over $100K a year, you want to look at changing your operation to an S-corp (not hard or expensive either) to avoid paying the 15% self-employment tax. I know guys operating an LLC and who make $400K a year and who pay $60K of that in self-employment tax. Switching from an LLC to an S-corp saved me a lot of money that I could spend elsewhere.

Banking

I use Bank of America and have a personal and business account. My brokerage pays my commissions via direct deposit to my business account. I have my business account pay my staff and me using QuickBooks payroll (super easy to set up and operate). My payroll checks from QuickBooks are direct-deposited into my personal account, and I can see all my accounts from one login. I could take draws out of the business if I had to (I never have to) as I can just adjust how much I'm paying myself each 2-week pay period. QuickBooks online connects very easily to my business account making it easy for my bookkeeper to do her work.

Accounting and Bookkeeping

QuickBooks automatically pulls all my revenue and expenses out of my business bank account. My accountant does my monthly bookkeeping (very inexpensive because it's mostly automated). Each month she asks me what category a few expenses would fall into that she didn't recognize, and I spend about 10 minutes on this work. Because she does the bookkeeping, I know and pay my quarterly taxes, and at the end of the year it takes me about an hour's worth of time versus when I was an unorganized sole proprietor—it would take me days to organize and report stuff to my accountant.

Payroll

QuickBooks online connects easily to my banking account, and I spend about five minutes every two weeks operating it. It is amazingly easy to set up and use.

Learn to Budget Expenses

One of the steps you need to take right away when you open for business is to create a budget. Your first three months will be crucial if you don't have a lot of cash in reserve. You can find many available Excel templates to track a budget. You are a small business now, and you must track your spending and make sure you can cover all your personal and business expenses. Once you get rolling, you'll keep tracking expenses, and you can easily get profit and loss statements from your accounting software. This business is great, I went from nothing to averaging $12,500 a month in my first year to $20,000 a month in my second year and so on…

Financial Planning

Now is the time to interview financial planners. It's a smart idea to take recommendations from wealthy friends. You will start making good money before you know it and must have a solid plan for it.

Real Estate Contracts

Focus on learning your contract inside and out. It is at the core of what we do for our clients. We wear 10 hats, but the main one is representing our clients and working through our contracts. If I hire a new agent, they must learn the contracts first; many are learning the contract while they are still taking pre-licensing classes.

Your Database/Sphere of Influence

We love Followup boss. It's scalable and a useful place to add your sphere of influence. You will soon be deciding on how you'll contact your database and how many times you must reach out to them.

Growing a Team

Read *The Millionaire Real Estate agent* by Gary Keller. It's the best book out there to give you step by step instructions to grow from a single agent to a team and then a Mega Team. I enjoy watching team members grow financially, start families and become very successful. My commission plans are designed to build loyalty and not squeeze every nickel for myself. This strategy has served me well with little turnover, motivated quality agents, and continued financial growth for all of us.

Technology Essentials That Work

Armed with knowledge from years of trial and error with systems that didn't live up to their sales rep's promises or flat out didn't work, we have created a system that runs smooth, is scalable with our growth, and works wonderfully. The technology you choose will have a large impact on your success. Your contact management software, website, email blast software, and many other applications will assist you in standing out in your market.

Website: Real Geeks (realgeeks.com)

Our Real Geeks website is affordable, and our cost per lead comes in at around $15-40. Most sites are similar in that they are going to deliver the same type of lead, so for us, it's about getting that cost per lead to a number that makes sense. When you cut through all the marketing bullshit, it comes down to cost per lead. It's easy to make changes to the site; they have a nice backend and a cool tool to automate Facebook advertisements. They have an in-house marketing team that manages our pay-per-click advertising and keeps our cost per lead down. The site is mobile optimized, fully responsive, SEO-friendly, a cinch to customize, and packed with easy-to-use features. The system creates great market reports, has agent landing pages for team members, and uses a clean and professional design. We love this company. There are other platforms like placester.com that are an affordable choice. Curaytor.com is good for small teams and commissionsinc.com and boomtown.com have great reputations for larger teams. I'd check them all out and see which one fits you best.

CRM, Lead Aggregation, Drip Email. Our Hub: Followupboss: (followupboss.com)

Followupboss allows us to connect with and collect all our leads in one place. FUB integrates with and can collect leads from over 200 lead sources. The system instantly assigns leads to agents based on the rules and flow we choose and specify, including price, zip code, etc. Followupboss responds instantly upon receiving leads by sending a personalized text and email which results in us getting a high response rate from our leads on the text element alone. It provides a CRM for each agent on my team, drip email, and fantastic customer support. I hear others rave about contractually.com, and nimble.com.

Landing Page Tool: Unbounce (unbounce.com)

If our website is our infantry, our landing pages are our special forces. Unbounce Landing pages look awesome, are easy to deploy, and have great lead capture tools. This tool allows us to build high-converting landing pages easily and those leads flow automatically into Followupboss and auto distribution to the groups that should get them. These landing pages are easy to take from idea to implementation. It has a simple interface. We love this company.

A couple of our landing pages:

- **The Maryland Equity Guard**: theequityguard.com
- **Towns at Eager Park**: townsateagerpark.com

Email Marketing: MailChimp (mailchimp.com)

MailChimp connects to our Followupboss database, and it's easy to segment our database using all sorts of different parameters and send and track campaigns. Who doesn't love this company?

Email Blast: Madmimi (madmimi.com)

Madmimi offers an easy way to send quick and easy email blasts to the agent database for our broker open houses. Very effective.

3D Tours: Matterport (matterport.com)

This is the industry standard for 3-D Tours. We created a virtual reality program using a Samsung headset for one of our large builder clients.

Email Management: SaneBox (sanebox.com)

This is an amazing email filter. I cannot remember life before SaneBox. It's a must use.

Free Live Streaming App: Periscope (pscp.tv)

We use this to walk remote buyers through houses. It works great.

E-Signature service: DocuSign (docusign.com)

DocuSign enables electronic signatures, and it works great.

Cloud File Storage: Dropbox (dropbox.com)

This is an easy-to-use, multi-platform, document storage site. You can share folders with other Realtors and clients.

Note Sharing: Evernote (evernote.com)

Capture, organize and share notes from anywhere with Evernote. Your best ideas are always with you and always in sync. Great for writing a book!

Technology, like medicine, is always changing, and it will keep you on your toes. All the solutions we use and the others we suggest are all good choices for making your technology picks less confusing.

RON'S RULES FOR THE DRIVER'S SEAT:

- Make your brand stand out.
- Adopt a performance mindset.
- Connect better with those around you.
- Focus on creating friends, not funnels.
- With the goal of strengthening your friendship, reconnect with everyone you know.
- Build your sphere: Get involved in the community.
- Throw or sponsor as many events a year as you can.

- Invite new and old friends and clients to all your events.
- Do social media right.
- Pick an office you love.
- Get your banking, accounting, and business set up straight.
- You are a small business. It will be hard to succeed working less than 40 hours a week.
- After you have reconnected with everyone you know, connect with eight people a day, or 56 a week. These connections can be friends, past clients, old leads or new prospects. Just do it.

Business Planning & Tracking

Just like any business, you'll need a business plan, a daily success tracker and a way to track your key business numbers. You will have to get really good at generating, tracking and following up with leads and you will also need to master working with buyers and sellers. You should focus on a six month, 1-year and a 5-year plan. You'll need to figure your personal, family, spiritual and social objectives so everything aligns. Once you've set all your goals, it's helpful to have someone hold you accountable. If you've owned a successful small business in the past, this will all make sense. If being a Realtor is your first small business, you might consider hiring a coach to help you make all the best moves. There are a range of coaching options out there; it's about finding the right fit for you and your business.

Keep learning at: createdemandandstopchasing.com

Chapter 9

Your Journey to the Top

"Only those who dare to fail greatly can ever achieve greatly."
-Robert F. Kennedy

I remain focused on providing a great service and building a successful business. The concepts I've shared with you are the ones I've used to get and stay at the top of my market.

For some of you, success will come quickly using these ideas, for others it will take more time.

If you transformed into the best version of yourself, adopted a performance mindset, focused on being a better friend, and got involved with the community while building your sphere it would be highly likely you would generate transactions and get your business off the ground. You will need to do a bunch of other stuff to build your business, too, and here are some more tips.

10 Additional Ways You Can Generate Business Fast Without the Chase.

1. Meet with all the busy agents in your office. Convince them you can take care of any of their overflow for a fair referral fee. This works great, many of the newer agents do this in our office.

2. Partner 50/50 with a lender and buy leads from Zillow. This is a 6-month commitment but can work if you target the right zip codes.

3. Use a website. Use Google AdWords to promote your website and capture leads. We use a Real Geeks website (there are plenty of other good ones), and they offer an AdWords service, all for a good price.

4. Partner with a lender and title company and put on a monthly home buying seminar. Promote and target it on Facebook.

5. Use a nice listing (with permission) from your office and do a promoted post on Facebook targeting an area and income bracket that makes sense.

6. Capture seller leads with a home valuation site. Promote on Facebook and Google AdWords. We use homevalueleads.com and are happy with their results.

7. Take up new hobbies to meet people. We have kickball, softball, football, and all sorts of leagues in our area. Join a running group, a book club, or join a group on meetup.com.

8. Remember the entire chapter on giving back to your community? If you have time, give back even more. This is by far the best way to connect with people while doing good.

9. Do open houses on busy streets and promote on Facebook.

10. Promote a landing page on Facebook.

11. Bonus idea. We had an agent that met people on match.com and then would meet those person's friends and sell them houses. Try this one at your own risk.

RON'S RULES FROM THE TOP:

- The more demand you create, the less lead gen work you'll have to do.
- Create Demand and find another 5-10 ways to generate business.
- If you like what you've learned, but also want to chase business, you're in luck. There are plenty of trainings to choose from.

Keep learning at: createdemandandstopchasing.com

Chapter 10

Cleared for Takeoff

"The journey of a thousand miles begins with one step"
-Lao Tzu

You now know my story. Now it's time to improve yours. Encountering my dilemmas, while at my lowest point on that couch, has proven to be the best thing to happen to me. Getting close to hitting rock bottom forced me to take action and get a handle on my life so that I could grow into a top producer in my community.

I was fortunate to have plenty of positive influences throughout my life who inspired me when I needed it most. If it weren't for Coach Hampe on that first day of school, I would never have learned the massive effort it takes to implement anything that's worth working toward. No more half-assed workdays. Learning from my friend the importance of being seen as *sharp like a pilot* proved to be more beneficial than I initially thought. Despite surviving the previously mentioned minor brush with death in flight school, I recently gained a new client who wanted my business because I'm a pilot. I am grateful to the doctor I met in Waikiki who taught me that just because you've been in a profession for years, it doesn't mean you know it all. You are always practicing, whether it's discovering safer ways to perform surgery or keeping up with the smart methods of sharing on social media.

Even with my real estate success, I'm not one to coast, and I don't want to hoard what I've learned. So, I hope you take these lessons, tactics, and ideas, and incorporate them into your routine. I've read enough flimsy training books to know exactly what real estate agents and small business owners need to launch their businesses or take them to the next level.

Make Your Brand the Best Version of Yourself

Simply put, get your brand straight by creating the best version of who you are. Whether you're just starting out, or have been established for a while and are working on rebranding, your reputation and what you stand for impact whether you get hired or passed over. You don't get any points or commission checks for coming in second!

My brand is tough to compete with; I'm sharp like a pilot; I'm the hardest working Realtor who starts his day at 5 a.m.; I'm all about the relationship, not the sale; I have a performance mindset, and I'm super involved in the community. It works. It stands out, and it gets me hired...a lot. If I can quote one of those popular big brands: *Just do it*. Take a hard look at yourself, identify your problems, and get rid of them. Then you'll stop losing business to higher-producing agents.

Adopt a High-Performance Mindset

Imagine, if like a pilot, you treated everything as if your life depended on it. You'd do things correctly and completely every single time, make better decisions every single time, and put first things first every single time.

Find out when your mind is at its sharpest during the day (or night) and optimize your work hours around it. Stop taking shortcuts; they can kill your career and your motivation. Visualize your successful day and plan to bring the calm wherever it is needed.

Focus on communicating better with those around you, and don't let your emotions take over. Make your intentions clear. Be prepared to deal with the unexpected and don't panic when you can't prevent shit from hitting the fan. You can do this by learning to manage your stress with relaxation techniques, practicing yoga, or doing whatever works to *become* the stress reliever. Like a pilot's lifesaving checklist put the important things first and go from there. When you implement just a few of these mindsets, your business will soar.

Use Your Knowledge of Mental Triggers for Good

The question we all have: How can you make people like you and want to hire you? You're always selling, but here is how you do it without a pitch. Simply focus on these extremely powerful concepts and use them responsibly. Become known as an authority in your market and know your shit. Be generous with your friends, acquaintances, neighborhood, and city to create reciprocity. Throwing events that mix past customers with new friends is a great way to create social proof. Put on memorable events regularly, and you will build a community that anticipates the ritual of getting together. Not smothering or annoying your friends creates scarcity and anticipation. People will want to see you. Make your actions predictable, and you will build trust. Become the best version of yourself, and your likeability will expand.

Don't Push People You Know Down Sales Funnels

As I said before, if you focus on sincere friendships, the business will follow. You should also volunteer as much as your schedule allows so that you can meet great people. You'll generate more business, become a better person, help a cause, and shine a brighter light on our industry when you invest in relationships and give back to the community.

Be Aware of Your Social Media Presence

Like anything in technology and online, the methods that work today aren't going to work tomorrow.

Before you hit the "post" button run through the possible mental triggers: authority, reciprocity, social proof, community, rituals, likeability, trust, scarcity, and anticipation. Don't try and go viral.

Get off the Ground Fast

Reconnecting with and sharing the new you with everyone you know can be key to jumpstarting your business. Setting up your business the right way will save you tens of thousands of dollars once you are making money and picking proven technology that works will make your business hum.

Now What?

The next steps are up to you. Focus on your brand. Work on your mindset. Become a noble Jedi by responsibly using mental triggers. Treat relationships like they matter (because they do). Take your social media seriously and get your business in order.

I started out at my lowest point on a couch, one shitty day. If you're reading this, you're already way ahead of where I was at that point. But you'll have to climb some walls and run through obstacles. As you assess who you are and what you're capable of, you'll need to strip away the layers of bullshit that we all tell ourselves. This won't be easy. Achieving crystalline clarity never is. Keep learning at: createdemandandstopchasing.com

Helpful Realtor Resources

Great Podcasts

1. Pat Hiban's Real Estate Rockstar Radio:
   hibandigital.com

2. Keeping It Real
   keepingitreal.com

3. Agent Caffeine
   agentcaffeine.com

4. Real Estate Coaching Radio
   blogtalkradio.com/realestatecoaching

5. Unlisted with Brad Inman
   soundcloud.com/inmannews

6. Caravan Confessions
   soundcloud.com/caravanconfessions

Must-Reads for Realtors

1. *The Millionaire Real Estate Agent* by Gary Keller

2. *7L: The Seven Levels of Communication: Go from Relationships to Referrals* by Michael J. Maher

3. *The Miracle Morning for Real Estate Agents: It's Your Time to Rise and Shine* by Hal Elrod and Michael J. Maher

4. *The Conversion Code: Capture Internet Leads, Create Quality Appointments, Close More Sales* by Chris Smith

5. *Crush It! Why NOW is the Time to Cash in on Your Passion* by Gary Vaynerchuk

6. *6 Steps to 7 Figures: A Real Estate Professional's Guide to Building Wealth and Creating Your Own Destiny* by Pat Hiban

7. *The ONE Thing: The Surprisingly Simple Truth Behind Extraordinary Results* by Gary Keller and Jay Papasan

References

1. Cialdini, Robert. *Influence: The Psychology of Persuasion.* New York, NY: Harper Collins, 1984.

2. Covey, Stephen R. *The 7 Habits of Highly Effective People.* New York, NY: Simon & Schuster LTD, 2013.

3. Dweck, Carol. *Mindset: The New Psychology of Success.* New York, NY: Random House, 2006.

4. Walker, Jeff. *Launch: An Internet Millionaire's Secret Formula to Sell Almost Anything Online, Build a Business You Love, and Live the Life of Your Dreams.* New York, NY: Morgan James Publishing, 2014.

5. Friel, Joe. *The Cyclist's Training Bible.* New York, NY: Velo Press, 2009.

6. Ideonomy. Accessed May 06, 2018. http://ideonomy.mit.edu/essays/traits.html

7. Sarikas, Christine. "129 Great Examples of Community Service Projects." Should You Go to College? 4 Pros and 3 Cons. Accessed May 06, 2018. https://blog.prepscholar.com/129-examples-of-community-service-projects.

About the Author

Ron Howard is a top Realtor in Baltimore and the recipient of the RE/MAX Circle of Legends award in recognition of his career accomplishments. Over the past six years, Ron Howard & Associates has sold over $549 million in sales with over $155 million in 2016, making them the #1 sales team in Baltimore city/county. Ron's team holds the rare distinction of being both the highest-ranked selling team in Baltimore and the most favorably reviewed, as his team ranked 65th in *The Wall Street Journal's* top teams in the USA for 2015. Ron has, year after year, earned RE/MAX's highest annual sales award—the Diamond Club—while also being inducted into their Hall of Fame and receiving their Lifetime Achievement award.

Ron became a real estate professional after he and a partner bought, renovated, and sold dozens of properties. He's built upon his professional experiences in sales, information technology, broadcast video production, and computer networking—from which he learned how to launch innovative, high-impact marketing campaigns. A cornerstone accomplishment was creating and launching Proforms, a contract writing software for the residential real estate industry. His specialty in the technology of automating workgroups and workflow has bolstered his success in pioneering a team approach to the real estate business.

Firmly dedicated to the city of Baltimore, Ron serves as a board or committee member for a few well-regarded nonprofits, as he focuses on the betterment of the community through giving back.

Today, Ron's team is recognized in Baltimore and its surrounding communities as proven real estate professionals who counsel home buyers on current market trends, assist with property valuation and purchasing, and, through their exceptional negotiating skills, achieve the best price and contractual terms for the sellers they represent.

As an FAA licensed private pilot with a passion for flying, Ron belongs to the Aircraft Owners and Pilots Association and in his free time enjoys mountain biking and snowboarding.

Professional memberships include the NAR, MAR, and GBBR.

Get in touch with Ron at:

Facebook.com/groups/createdemandandstopchasing
Twitter.com/ronhowardrealty
Youtube.com/rhanetwork
Instagram: @rhanetwork

Nonprofits We Like

1. Ronald McDonald House Charities

   rmhc.org

2. Believe in Music

   webelieveinmusic.com

3. Kennedy Krieger Institute – Project Heal

   kennedykrieger.org/community/maryland-center-developmental-disabilities/project-heal

4. Living Classrooms Foundation

   livingclassrooms.org

5. Believe in Tomorrow

   believeintomorrow.org

6. Baltimore Youth Cycling

   baltimoreyouthcycling.org

7. Friends of Patterson Park

   pattersonpark.com

8. Saint Francis Neighborhood Center
   stfranciscenter.org

9. International Mountain Bicycling Association
   imba.com

Online Course Offer

Free Online Course Module for Relationship-Building Science

Sign up for free instant access to our Relationship-Building Science module, part of our Create Demand and Stop Chasing Business online course at: relationshipbuildingscience.com.

Join our Community

Join our community where we can all share great ideas at facebook.com/groups/createdemandandstopchasing.

Learn to Fly

Flight training is an amazing journey and can enrich your life in countless ways. As discussed, you'll adopt a new performance mindset and have the best time of your life. For more information and to find a flight school near you, visit: aopa.org

Take care - Ron

CPSIA information can be obtained
at www.ICGtesting.com
Printed in the USA
BVHW04s1256110918
527174BV00012B/105/P